Development
Planning in Ireland

**PRAEGER SPECIAL STUDIES IN
INTERNATIONAL ECONOMICS AND DEVELOPMENT**

Development
Planning in Ireland

Loraine Donaldson

FREDERICK A. PRAEGER, Publishers
New York · Washington · London

The purpose of the Praeger Special Studies is to make specialized research monographs in U.S. and international economics and politics available to the academic, business, and government communities. For further information, write to the Special Projects Division, Frederick A. Praeger, Publishers, 111 Fourth Avenue, New York, N.Y. 10003.

FREDERICK A. PRAEGER, PUBLISHERS
111 Fourth Avenue, New York, N.Y. 10003, U.S.A.
77-79 Charlotte Street, London W.1, England

Published in the United States of America in 1966
by Frederick A. Praeger, Inc., Publishers

Library of Congress Catalog Card Number: 66-14087

Printed in the United States of America

*To the Memory
of my Father*

ACKNOWLEDGMENTS

This study was possible because of the open-hearted friendliness and helpfulness of many, many people in the Republic of Ireland—in government, in business, in education, and in private life. In no way, however, are those who cooperated responsible for the interpretations and contents of the study.

The aid received and favors done were so numerous that it is impossible to name a few names without slighting many. But I must mention with gratefulness Mr. A. A. Pakenham-Walsh of Trinity College, Dublin, and the Doyles of Baggot Street. Mr. Pakenham-Walsh was my first contact on the island, and was of invaluable assistance. Mrs. Emily Doyle and her daughter, Clodagh, took me into their home when I was seriously ill in a strange land, and I was little more than a stranger to them.

My deep appreciation goes to Professors Robert C. Turner, Stefan H. Robock, and L. L. Waters of Indiana University. Their criticisms and suggestions have been invaluable, and their interest and encouragement a source of strength. Professor J. Potter of the United Kingdom was also especially kind and helpful in devoting time to improving my work. Special thanks go to Professor Paul Gordon, who helped establish contacts in Ireland, and to John Prior Lewis, whose ideas and insights, gained while his research assistant and student at Indiana University, influenced my work in so many different ways.

Vari-typing of the manuscript was done by Mrs. Kathryn Bailey of Atlanta, Georgia, and I am grateful to her for a skillful, professional job.

I also wish to acknowledge the money received from the Ford Foundation which made this study possible.

Loraine Donaldson

Atlanta, Georgia

CONTENTS

LIST OF TABLES

Development
Planning in Ireland

1

PLANNING IN A
TRANSITION ECONOMY

The truth is we are all planners now....
In fact, the central issue...is not
whether there shall be planning, but
what form it shall take....[1]

AN UNLIKELY CANDIDATE

Possessed of a legendary contradictory nature, a fervent devotion to freedom, and a tendency to find glory in the past, the Irish were not likely candidates for planning. After all, planning is a design of internal consistency, oriented toward the future. And it can bring with it restrictions upon actions long accustomed to unrestricted freedom.

But there were pressures upon Ireland from within and without—pressures in the form of new trading blocks, high emigration rates, and unemployment in a stagnant economy. There was an economic vacuum in the area of industrial development. The government stepped in, but not too far. It has planned, but not too much. And the description of planning adopted in Ireland is, according to some, a contradiction in terms. For, the Irish speak of their programming efforts as "democratic" planning.

Like development planning in many other countries around the globe, planning in Ireland is a pragmatic innovation designed to guide an economy that had not spontaneously coordinated its economic action so as to achieve economic development. The desire of the Irish for development was plainly discernible in the silent protest of those leaving the island—an island nestled along the periphery of Europe's expanding prosperity, but failing to share in the rising living standards of countries with which it traded. External stimulus in the form of Britain's proposed entry into the European Economic Community interacted with internal discontent to shake the Irish loose from the lethargy of the past and move them boldly into the formulation of long-range plans for the nation's future.

Today the Republic of Ireland, after six years of planning, is well on her way to proving that she can achieve reasonably rapid economic development. Ireland has implemented her planning strategy through government action of a relatively indirect nature aimed at increasing private investment, and through the redirection of public investment in accordance with a coordinated plan for expansion. This study analyzes the achievement of industrialization goals during the successful first six years of planning, focusing specifically upon the implementation tools set up to achieve economic performance in line with plan objectives.

IMPLEMENTATION OF PLANNING

Certain types and certain mixes of investment control tools have become acceptable and seemingly important control mechanisms of governments seeking to influence market economies. In manipulating economies of a decentralized character to achieve established objectives, governments have typically resorted to credit controls, interest rate changes, subsidies on desired investment, tax exemption for increasing investment, and in areas of acceptability, government enterprise.

Ireland has been no exception to this generalization. Moreover, planning in Ireland is highly similar to the French postwar planning which relies upon controls of the above types:

> At its inception, the system has definitely been helped by the fact that France already had a kind of mixed economy in which about one half of gross investment originates with the public sector or is directly controlled by it. It has a large state owned industrial sector.... The government has maintained direct control over the credit system. Through the *Credit National*, for instance, which is a private bank whose operations are controlled by the state, nationalized industries and private companies complying with the objective of the Plan can get cheaper loans than on the open market.[2]

Both the French and the Irish emphasize the "democratic" form of their planning. The main characteristics of the variety of planning used in France and Ireland which are referred to as giving the planning process a "democratic" nature are: decentralization of goal setting through consultation with industry; the setting of non-punitive targets, these targets being at the industry level rather than the firm level; reliance upon indirect control measures by government to manipulate the economy, e.g., credit control and subsidies[3]; and the absence of need for a large network of governmental machinery to draw up or follow through on plan goals. Where there is consensus in a society concerning the need for a certain degree of long-range planning, yet support for planning exists only to the extent that it is compatible with a market economy, the French approach to planning accommodates the situation.

Ireland has officially declared preference for a predominantly private market economy in reflection of the sentiment of the populace. However, the industrial sector is relatively undeveloped in Ireland and the government investment program over the first six years of planning accounted for approximately half of total investment. Thus, despite official commitment to a market economy, and the desire to see the private sector's share of investment rise, at the present level of industrial development Ireland's capital formation pattern is shaped more by her level of industrialization than her economic organizational preferences.

Since a large segment of investment was government investment at the inception of planning, the level of public investment was one route by which Ireland could achieve plan goals without introducing additional centralization of the economy. Two other major means by which she chose to approach plan implementation via influence of investment were the use of government subsidies and government credit. Precedence was also well established for the use of these latter instruments, as well as the instrument of government enterprise.

Ireland has been surprised by her own success in the attainment of growth goals. Her first program's growth target of a 2 per cent per annum increase in real output was exceeded 100 per cent. The steady expansion of the Irish economy at somewhat above 4 per cent a year has been spurred by the 7 per cent rate of growth of the industrial sector.

GOVERNMENT CONTROL AND INFLUENCE OF INVESTMENT

As previously noted, this study examines the importance of government influence and control of investment in achieving goals of industrialization established under the Irish development programs. More specifically, the study breaks down into four elements:

1. Identification of the economic background leading up to economic planning, and the strategy of economic expansion outlined under the First and Second Expansion programs.

2. Identification of the machinery of investment planning and implementation in Ireland.

3. Establishment of the progress toward industrialization during the period from mid-1958 to mid-1964, as defined and sought by the First and Second Expansion programs, and the extent of government influence and control over industrial investment that occurred during this period.

4. Analysis and appraisal of the composition of the mix of dominant implementation tools used by the Irish government to induce new investment.

There are important limitations to a study of this nature. There is no general theory of economic development, and thus cause-effect reasoning is limited. The study does not attempt to analyze the strategy or design for industrialization that the Irish planners have chosen, nor to develop criteria from which to evaluate the results of the planning as realized to date. General goals toward which the plans are aimed that are highly influenced by new industrial investment—such as a dramatic increase in industrial production as a per cent of GNP—are uncritically accepted, and their achievement is considered synonymous with plan success.

Concentration is placed upon new investment as a measure of plan success. There are several reasons for this. New plant and equipment spending is a prime indicator of industrialization. It is through influencing new investment spending that the Irish are implementing their plan goal of industrialization. Alternative measurements of industrialization, such as contribution to GNP of new operations in the industrial sector, or employment in manufacturing, would not be satisfactory indicators because the study is confined to the first six years of planning in Ireland. As a result, new firms in a great many cases were operating below anticipated normal output and employment levels in their first year or two of operation.

In sum, in answering the question how important government influence and control of investment are in Irish development planning, the government's strategy and the goals of planning are accepted, and the importance of investment per se in achieving plan goals such as increased industrial output is assumed. It is the government's role in promoting and inducing investment which is under study.

Within limits, the government's influence over state enterprise is fairly easily established. The roles of tax exemption, government grants, and government credit are not easily isolated as determinants of new investment and thus instruments in the achievement of program targets of increased industrial activity. Yet, an attempt is made to extricate the importance of such implementation tools as tax exemption from the general assortment of policy measures designed to promote development goals. In doing so, an argument is developed for the conclusion that policies other than those specifically examined were helpful, often necessary contributors to increasing the pace of industrial investment, but were not prime or sufficient causes for the increase of new firms over the past six years in Ireland. The courage to attempt to isolate the effects of tax exemption is gained from the following plea of Richard Goode:

> The efficiency of tax exemption has been widely debated, but much less effort has gone into detailed appraisal of actual experience. The difficulties encountered in such a study are formidable, but perhaps no greater than in empirical investigations of other important tax questions.[4]

DESIGN OF THE STUDY

Several months were spent in Ireland gathering first-hand information on the implementation of the Irish expansion programs. Published and unpublished statistics and written materials were obtained from government and other sources. Interviews were obtained with the Central Statistics Office, the Planning Agency, government agencies responsible for plan implementation, the Federation of Irish Industries, and economists and other informed individuals inside and outside of the government in an effort to assemble both background information and information specific to the aspect of planning under study. Wherever possible, more than one source was used for obtaining information of central pertinence to the study in order to avoid bias. Naturally, not all information sought was available—either because it was non-existent or not obtainable. Fortunately no glaring gaps occurred in needed data.

Preliminary investigation led to the conclusion that the government's role in implementing plan goals for industrialization of the economy had been concentrated upon the control and influence of investment. More direct and detailed study established the fact that new industrial investment influenced or controlled by the government was roughly three-fourths of total new fixed capital formation in the industrial sector. The study then turned to careful examination and support of the statement that government subsidies in the form of non-repayable cash grants and tax exemption, government credit, and government enterprise were the main implementation tools used by the Irish government to induce new industrial investment—particularly investment in the strategic export sector—and that these tools were playing a major role in inducing new industrial activity in the economy.

Establishment of the government's influence and control of public investment to achieve plan goals was a fairly straightforward matter. The first step was to identify the percentage of new fixed capital formation in the industrial sector accounted for by public enterprise to determine whether government enterprise did in fact play an important role in the economy. The second step was to show the general pattern of public investment over the planning period under observation in relation to the general goals of industrialization set forth in the programs for economic expansion. The third step was to examine the political-economic implications of government enterprise as a tool of plan implementation and a major component of the implementation mix.

Since the plan goals for public investment were set forth in general terms —the change of emphasis from social investment such as housing to investment in production facilities such as fertilizer—government success in attaining these goals was not difficult to isolate. An analysis in depth of the economic performance of the public enterprise in the Irish environment is outside the scope of this study. A detailed study of the economic record of Irish public enterprises, however, would be a highly desirable extension of knowledge about the Irish economy, and could help to substantiate or refute the preliminary conclusions of this study concerning the role the wholly owned and/or mixed public-private enterprises should play in Ireland's future industrial growth.

From the standpoint of empirical evidence, the major emphasis of the study has been placed upon examination of the role of government subsidies in inducing new industrial capital formation. Early in the study it became apparent that credit by the government to encourage new industry played a lesser role than subsidies, and often was granted along with subsidies to the same firms. A questionnaire was designed to test the influence of subsidies upon new investment, and included the influence of credit upon new investment within its scope.

The interview form was limited in length so that it could be adequately filled out in twenty minutes if the executive were unwilling to grant more time. The fact that the form was short facilitated the interview in two ways: it seemed to increase the care with which each question was answered, and thus the accuracy, and it allowed interviews to be set up when executives were unwilling to spare more than twenty minutes of their time.

There was a tendency for firms to be hesitant in granting interviews on two counts: the confidential status of information that might be desired, and the anticipation of difficult questions which could not be answered. In requesting interviews, then, the simplicity of questions in relation to available information any firm would record was stressed. Also, assurance was given, and put in writing where desired, that all information would be confidential in that it would not be identified with the firm interviewed. As a result, response to initial requests for interviews of twenty minutes was excellent, and actual interviews were granted that lasted up to a half-day.

The questionnaire consisted of 14 questions as follows:

1. Name of firm.

2. Address.

3. Products produced.

4. Annual sales.

5. Percentage of sales outside Ireland.

6. Number of employees.

7. Investment in plant and equipment since 1957.

8. Type of government investment subsidy.

9. Approximate size of subsidy.

10. If foreign firm, what part of the subsidy is cancelled by taxation in home country?

11. What important factors influenced your investment decision?

12. (Ranking of factors from Number 11 on grid.)

13. Would you have invested without government subsidies?

14. Do you expect to continue operations after expiration of the effects of the subsidy (e.g., tax exemption)?

Number 9, approximate size of subsidy, was answered by some firms who were willing to give the amount of grants received. Many firms were unwilling or unable to estimate tax relief subsidies. The heart of the questionnaire was contained in Question 11 regarding the reasons for investment. After executives identified the main factors influencing their decision to invest in new plant and equipment, they were asked to rank these factors, along with government subsidies if subsidies were not named as an important factor, on a four-point grid as "very important," "important," "of little importance," and "of no importance."

No suggestions were made to influence the executive's reply. He was asked to name the important factors that had played a part in bringing about his firm's new investment. Then, if tax exemption, industrial credit, or grants were not mentioned, he was asked if they played a role, and what role. If there seemed to be inconsistencies in the answers, further questions were asked in an attempt to clear them up. No illusion was entertained, however, that all investment decisions were necessarily logically consistent or rational.

To facilitate recording the answers to Question 12, expected determinants of new investment—accessibility to the United Kingdom market and to other European markets, low-cost labor, available or skilled labor, grants, government credit, tax exemption, government-trained personnel, government contacts, and access to raw materials—were typed on the form so they could be checked in the appropriate space according to rank of importance. Lines were provided to write in other factors influencing new investment and space was also left at the end of the questions to record pertinent comments made by the interviewees during the course of the interview.

The population from which the interview sample was drawn was made up of firms that had invested in plant and equipment since planning began in 1958. The large majority of firms accounting for new investment in Ireland during the period 1958-64 received tax remission combined with government grants and/or government credit. Moreover, there were few firms on the list, according to government officials, that did not have one of the three: tax remission, government grants, or government credit.

Firms accounting for new investment in Ireland over the period of the study consisted of 133 new firms with foreign participation, 55 new Irish firms, and 20 firms receiving adaptation grants to enable them to acquire plant and machinery needed to make them competitive in export trade. The latter group of 20 firms consisted of Irish firms and a few firms with foreign ownership claims. This list of firms receiving adaptation grants was necessarily incomplete because the information was not officially available; names of firms were obtained from various unofficial sources.

Ireland was represented by ownership claims in approximately 35 per cent of the total population. By pounds of investment, foreign capital dominated the list. Approximately 80 per cent of new-firm investment was accounted for by firms with foreign ownership. Among the 133 new firms with foreign participation, representation by countries was as follows: United Kingdom, 36 per cent; Germany, 27 per cent; United States, 24 per cent; and Holland, 5 per cent. Other countries represented by ownership claims in from one to four firms were Italy, Denmark, France, South Africa, Austria, Belgium, Japan, Israel, Canada, and Sweden.

Foreign firms locating in Ireland to export produced a diversified array of products. Although excavation equipment and fork-lift trucks for export were produced, other products were lighter in weight, and were goods with relatively low transportation costs. No one industry or group of industries dominated new investment in Ireland over the past six years. However, the following categories of new firm production provide a convenient grouping for describing the population. Yarn, carpets, clothing, and textiles were produced by 27 out of the total of 133 new firms with foreign participation established since 1958. Processed agricultural products (food, drink, etc.) were produced by 14 new firms with foreign participation, and the area of metal products, which includes such diverse goods as heaters, pipes, aluminum pots, and wire screens, accounted for 14 new firms. Products derived from wood were well represented, totaling 8 new firms manufacturing such products as veneers, packaging materials, paper products, and paper. There were 7 firms producing machinery, 6 plastic products, 5 cosmetics and pharmaceuticals, 4 electronic and electrical products, 2 chemicals, and 2 firms were set up to refine oil. The remaining firms represented a variety of industries.

A sample of 34 firms was taken from the population described above. A random sample rather than a stratified sample was chosen because, among the *a priori* factors that might have affected the role played by tax remission, grants, and government credit in inducing new investment, there was no one factor or two factors that dominated the list in such a way that a homogenous grouping could be derived. The sample of firms reflected the diversity of products of the population.

Firms interviewed were located in various areas over the island, although there was a concentration of interviews in Dublin County and at the Shannon Industrial Estate. This concentration was due partly to the occurrence of firms in these areas in the population, and partly to the fact that in arranging appointments it was often necessary to have intermediate contacts pave the way for access to top executives of the firms interviewed. Interviews were more successfully arranged in Dublin and surrounding areas because of the contacts there. It was felt that the small bias, if any, that might result from this concentration in location would be worth risking in order to obtain answers from executives who knew the background leading to the investment decision made by the firm. Executives with a rank of vice president (managing director in Ireland) or higher were contacted in almost all cases.

The number of times countries were represented by ownership (full ownership and part ownership) was as follows:

Country	Full Ownership	Joint Ownership
Ireland	7	4
United States	8	4
United Kingdom	5	1
Germany	3	
France	2	
Japan	1	
Belgium		1
Canada		1
Denmark	1	
Austria	1	
South Africa		1

Although American firms showed up heavily in the sample, there was no known bias working toward this result. The lack of representation of German firms compared to their occurrence in the population from which the sample was drawn is due to the difficulty experienced in arranging interviews with German firms. However, the three German executives with whom appointments were obtained were quite cooperative in divulging information and alloting time to the interview.

Early in the sampling it became evident that the results would establish an important place for tax exemption in the achievement of plan goals. The major determinants of new investment were government subsidies, markets, and labor, in that order. The results of the firm interviews are presented and analyzed in Chapter 6.

Notes

1. W. Arthur Lewis, *The Principles of Economic Planning,* Washington: Public Affairs Press, 1951, p. 14.

2. IMEDE *(l'Institut pour l'Etude des Methodes de Direction de l'Entreprise), Economic Planning in France,* Lausanne, Switzerland, 1962, p. 5.

3. J. M. Clark has written that controls tend to be acceptable to the extent that they are looked on "with the semi-unconsciousness of custom." (J. M. Clark, *Demobilization of Wartime Economic Controls,* New York: Mc-Graw-Hill Book Company, Inc., 1944, p. 49.) The ubiquity of controls of various types in any economy is pointed out by Dahl and Lindblom in *Politics, Economics and Welfare,* New York: Harper & Brothers, 1953, p. 54. The authors classify the social processes exerting control over economic life into four types: the price system, control by leaders (hierarchy), control over leaders (polyarchy), and control among leaders. The French planning technique utilizes the control of the market system and avoids the setting up of a conglomeration of hierarchical controls that the market economy is not accustomed to. This can be important to democratic support for planning in a country such as Ireland.

4. Richard Goode, "Taxation and Economic Development," *Readings in Economic Development,* Morgan, *et. al.,* (eds.), Belmont, California: Wadsworth Publishing Company, Inc., 1963, p. 381.

CHAPTER **2** PROFILE OF
IRELAND

Though native sons have fought over the island as if it were a blessed land, the Emerald Isle is not a "bit of heaven" for all Irishmen. Large numbers of emigrants have set sail from Ireland's shores to seek blessings of a type not found at home. Ireland was spoken of as the vanishing nation before the advent of planning in 1958, as members of the working age population who could not find employment left their native land in a steady stream.

CONFLICTS OF THE PAST

Formerly a part of the United Kingdom, Catholic Ireland fought for independence during the period 1918-21. After independence, the predominately Catholic counties formed a self-governing free state until 1948, when they became the Republic of Ireland. Northern Ireland, which consists of the six Protestant counties of Ulster and occupies about one-fifth of the northeastern portion of the Island, is still a part of the United Kingdom. Resentment over British domination during the seven and a half centuries prior to independence and over partition of the island with independence has occupied the energies of the people until recently. It was not until 1959 that a new style of leader (Sean Lemass) not preoccupied with partition and other old wounds came to power. "As *Fianna Fail's* new leader, Lemass was the antithesis of the old fire-breathing heroes, talked trade and tariffs to the voters."[1]

TASKS OF THE FUTURE

The island upon which the Republic of Ireland is situated receives an abundance of rainfall which contributes to the production of its primary product —grass. Not surprisingly, the main activity of the farming community is the production of grazing animals, to which 85 per cent of the country's agricultural land is devoted. In 1956, prior to the beginning of planning, 40 per cent of the working force was employed in agriculture (some being underemployed) and 28.9 per cent of the national income came from this source. Ireland's main export—her total exports run roughly 40 per cent of GNP—is live cattle which is shipped to Britain, her primary export market, to be fattened. In the past approximately 85 per cent by value of Ireland's exports have gone to Britain. The ability to achieve favorable terms of trade has been limited by dependence upon agricultural exports.

Ireland has no important natural resources other than agricultural resources. Inasmuch as her farms are being continuously forced to attain competitive levels of productivity, the number of employees that can be gainfully absorbed on the farms has been steadily declining. Programs to increase the use of fertilizer, introduce the widespread use of machinery, and combine small farms into economically viable units have all aggravated the unemployment problem in Ireland, despite their contribution to increased farm output.

The Republic of Ireland covers an area of 27,136 square miles, being larger than Belgium, Denmark, or Switzerland, but less than one-third the size of the United Kingdom or Western Germany. Inhabitants per square mile number a relatively meager 107, as compared to 753 in Belgium, 268 in Denmark, 312 in Switzerland, 541 in the United Kingdom, and 528 in Western Germany. Ireland's total population of 2.8 million has declined from a level around 8 million in the middle of the 19th century before the potato famine. There is only one city in Ireland, Dublin, with a population of over a hundred thousand people.

The task Ireland faces in trying to raise living standards and increase employment can be more fully appreciated by considering how greatly the American farm problem would be intensified if America's thinly populated agricultural states that lack non-agricultural resources were thrown back upon their own devices for providing a decent standard of living for the laborers leaving the farm. The analogy has other parallels. Americans are well-educated and expectant of achieving minimum standards of living. The Irish have been proud of their educational standards since the Dark Ages, when they helped to keep scholarship and learning alive in their monastaries and played a part in revitalizing Europe; and their exposure to English standards of living through occupation by the British and emigration to Britain have created desires and expectations of adequate living standards. Ireland's size and resource base may prohibit achievement of per capita incomes comparable to America, but, as the past six years have shown, vast improvements were possible beyond the level of an estimated 1956 per capita income of $423— as compared to $909 for Britain. [2]

The dependence of Ireland upon the United Kingdom market played a major role in the beginning of planning in Ireland, along with high emigration rates. When Britain decided to seek admission into the European Economic Community, it became apparent Ireland would have to follow, or be faced with losing her dominant export market, since Britain would be forced to conform to the common external tariff adhered to by all members of the Community. Moreover, even though Ireland should join the European Economic Community with Britain, her favored position in the British market would be gone. This realization at the time Britain applied for membership forced Ireland into a self-appraisal of her economy and its future. Out of this threat, and the alarm over a declining population, was born the will to cut tariffs, modernize existing industry, increase industrial production, and improve productivity in agriculture.

POLITICAL SUPPORT FOR PLANNING

The determination to place the conflicts of the past behind and work together for the future of Ireland as a country is reflected in the lack of basic differences in political parties. Besides *Fianna Fail* (Heroes of Destiny), there are two other principal parties in Ireland—*Fine Gael* and the Labor Party. The approach of the three parties toward planning involves differences in emphasis, rather than conflicts over whether or not there should be planning. The Labor Party, the smallest of the three principal parties, reminds the electorate it has long been vociferous in support of planning. It usually takes a stand for more government activity in the economy over existing levels. *Fine Gael* supports planning, but emphasizes the needs of agriculture rather than the need for rapid industrialization. *Fianna Fail* has been most often in power since 1932, and was led until 1959 by the revolutionary war hero de Valera. When Lemass took over in 1959, he chose to emphasize economic development, particularly the need for industrialization.

The Irish are proud of the highly developed institutions and procedures of a functioning democracy. The fact that Ireland possesses a highly developed democracy helped to determine the type of planning chosen. The Republic has a constitutional, parliamentary government with two houses, a president who is Head of State, and a prime minister who is Head of Government. Executive power rests with the prime minister as Head of Government, and the president acts on the advice and authority of the government. Members of the House of Representatives *(Dail)* are elected at least every five years by adult suffrage. The Senate consists of members appointed by the government and elected by various vocational and cultural groups. Its powers are highly circumscribed. The Senate may delay a bill for ninety days, or suggest changes, but cannot permanently block legislation. There is provision made in the constitution for the reference to the people of certain bills of national importance.

POPULATION AND LABOR FORCE[3]

As indicated above, the population of Ireland is very small, and its density is low. The population of the Republic of Ireland has been falling since the Great Famine of 1845-47, and in 1961 was 2.8 million, less than half of what it was in 1841. Since 1891 the population of Northern Ireland has risen slightly. Emigration lies behind the declining trend in population in the Republic of Ireland, rather than low birth rates or extremely high death rates.

The birth rate in Ireland is comparable to other European countries and that of the United States. The 1958-60 birth rate in Ireland was 21.1 per thousand population, compared to 17.1 for Belgium, 16.5 for Denmark, 18.2 for France and Italy, 16.7 for the United Kingdom, and 24.0 for the United States. The marriage rate is unusually low in Ireland, and the death rate comparable to that of the United Kingdom, which is relatively high compared to other European countries.

An explanation of the relatively high death rate can be found in the age structure of the population. Ireland has a high average age of population because of concentration in the older age group as a result of survival from a period when the absolute number of births was greater than it is now, and because of the tendency for emigrants to be concentrated primarily in the younger age group. Despite a natural increase in population of 9.3 per thousand in 1958-60, total population declined because of a rate of emigration of roughly 15 per thousand. At no time since 1871 have emigration rates been below 8.2 per thousand, except for the Great Depression years when lack of employment opportunities in other countries and restrictions upon immigration reduced the rate to 5.6 per thousand, and the years of World War II, when the rate was 6.3 per thousand.

The postwar years showed steady rises in emigration, and in 1957, 40,000 Irishmen a year left the homeland. This declined to an estimated 20,000 a year by 1964. The development plan goal calls for a reduction in emigration to around 10,000 a year by 1970. The United Kingdom, Canada, Australia, and the United States receive the majority of the Irish emigrants. Most of the out-migration is from the rural areas of Ireland.

Compared to other European countries, Ireland has a high proportion of the population in the dependent age groups, indicating that the costs of emigration are high indeed, since the productive years are lost. Many in the dependent group are on small, non-viable farms in the West of Ireland.

It is often the case that the more industrious and enterprising leave the country. One Irish economist has noted that,

> Emigration seems also to produce certain attitudes of mind and
> patterns of behavior which are prejudicial to economic development.
> People appear to become...like an uprooted or rootless people even
> in their own country. This results in a tendency to evade risk-taking

and responsibility so that even the limited investment opportunities
that exist are not exploited to the full.[4]

Moreover, the small population with a high dependency group, combined with
the low incomes of a dominantly agricultural society, have limited the home
market and made the goals of increased industrial employment highly dependent upon exports during the early years of expansion. Of course, once expansion takes place, incomes rise, and population increases with the decline of
emigration, development efforts can gain impetus from a growth in the home
market.

The total labor force declined from 1,305,000 in 1926 to 1,186,000 in
1958, and the total number at work fell from 1,220,000 in 1926 to 1,121,000 in
1958. Employment is estimated to have held steady since 1958. Agricultural
work is the largest single source of employment, although the proportion of the
work force engaged in agriculture declined from 46 per cent of the labor force
in 1946 to 38 per cent in 1958, and is continuing to decline as farms are
mechanized. Two categories, manufacturing, and commerce, insurance and
finance, absorbed the majority of workers leaving the farms over the past
forty years who did not emigrate. Jobs in manufacturing increased during the
period of protection when industries first developed, and in the post-1958
period when there was a large inflow of foreign capital and establishment of
new industries.

Education levels are high in Ireland; however the educational system is
not oriented toward the needs of an industrial society, and workers are often
unused to handling machinery or being subjected to the discipline of industrial work. Education for the professions, a reflection of status priorities, may
have contributed to emigration. The forces affecting emigration are complex,
and often reinforcing. The Irish are examining in what ways their educational
system can more readily contribute to a rise of living standards in Ireland and
a decline in out-migration through affecting the educational and skill mix of
the labor force as a whole.

STRUCTURE OF AGRICULTURE

Ireland long has been an agricultural adjunct of the United Kingdom.
About 50 per cent of what the farmer produces is sold on the export market,
mostly to Britain. Livestock and livestock products in 1954-59 composed about
77 per cent by pound value of farm output. Cattle, pigs, milk, and eggs accounted for the largest output by value in this category. Wheat, oats, barley,
sugar beets, potatoes, and turf (a peat type fuel) were the source of all but
roughly 3 per cent by value of farm output not originating from livestock
during this period.

The government is very active in the agricultural area, providing, e.g., marketing facilities, crop supports, fertilizer subsidization, land reclamation and farm building schemes, credit, advisory services, and education and research. Government efforts to increase output per worker in farming have been fairly successful. Over the past 10 years output per person engaged in farming increased by over 25 per cent in volume. Part of the increase is the result of decreased underemployment as a result of emigration from rural areas. Even though productivity has increased in agriculture, output per man and per acre have remained lower in Ireland than in many other European countries. The main reason for this is that Ireland has not yet mechanized the farms and organized for intensive production methods to the extent currently practiced in Europe.

The agriculture industry is characterized by a large number of small, and medium sized farms (30-100 acres), although the number of small holdings under 30 acres has declined since 1930. The number of farms 100 acres and larger has tended to remain constant. A large number of small farmers supplement their income when possible in other pursuits such as fishing, forestry, or road work.

The land in the West of Ireland is relatively poor, and the area is mainly occupied in sheep production. Dairying, pig production, and cattle raising characterize agricultural output in the South, and in the East the land is devoted to relatively more tillage and store and fat cattle.

The problems in agriculture are typical of those found in this sector in other countries. Incomes are low in relation to other sectors of the economy; the small marginal farmer is unwilling and/or unable to leave the agricultural way of life; foreign markets are limited by tendencies of other countries to subsidize and protect their farmers; and the trend toward mechanization demands the elimination of underemployment and the creation of jobs elsewhere in the economy to absorb migration from the rural area. The future of Ireland's agricultural sector is a question mark punctuating the uncertainties created by the realignment of trading blocks in Europe. Currently Ireland is a member of neither the European Free Trade Association nor the European Economic Community, although she has applied for membership in the latter. Optimists and pessimists speak out about the future of Irish agriculture should Ireland become a member of the European Economic Community, but political forces would play such a large part in deciding this future as to preclude accurate forecasting.

STRUCTURE OF INDUSTRY

Even before the first five-year expansion program in 1958, Ireland had progressed beyond most underdeveloped nations in reducing the level of dependence upon agriculture. Once free of British domination and civil strife, Ireland sought to encourage industrialization by a policy of protection. Protection was steadily built up during the 1930's, and the result has been a non-competitive industrial sector dependent upon a small protected home market. The philosophy surrounding this approach to industrialization is described as follows:

> Ireland made a late start in the industrial field. The lack of an industrial tradition, managerial skill, adequate risk capital, and native raw materials, with a heavily industrialized country as a close neighbor, made the new State's task of establishing industries particularly difficult. An extensive system of protective tariffs and quotas was needed to aid the infant industries and to overcome traditional consumer preferences, large scale advertising of British products and, in many cases, higher domestic costs of production.[5]

This selected route to industrialization seems to have had a particular shortcoming in Ireland with respect to the development of managerial talent. The level of income, and hence consumption, and the population size do not enable large-scale operations in most instances, nor does the market support enough firms in a given industry to provide domestic competition. The result has been a predominance of small, private firms internally held and run by tradition more than by principles of management. Contributing further to the acute shortage of entrepreneurial ability is the traditional lack of status attached to the businessman's functions in society. Ireland is a country that is 95 per cent Catholic, where a Catholic education is supported by the state. A career in the civil service or the professions has been more compatible with this educational background than the pursuit of profit.[6] As a result, many of Ireland's more talented people are in the government; or when they cannot find work commensurate with their educational aspirations and training, they have emigrated.

The inability for large numbers of job seekers to find remunerative managerial posts in the small, family-owned firm may be another reason many of Ireland's more talented individuals have been drawn to the civil service. The small size of the island, the scarcity of positions, and the interconnections in business, family, etc. work against mobility of personnel.

Prior to planning, the industrial sector output was dominated by a small group of industries. These are listed below, beside their ranking as sources of employment and contributors to GNP.

Product Category	Rank	
	Net Output	Source of Employment
Food	1	1
Metal & Engineering	2	2
Drink & Tobacco	3	6
Textiles	4	4
Paper & Printing	5	5
Clothing & Footware	6	3
Chemicals & Chemical Products	7	9
Clay Products, Glass, Cement, etc.	8	8
Wood & Furniture	9	7

Generally there has been diversification of the industrial base since 1958. An aircraft manufacturing plant is being set up. Two oil refining firms are now in operation. New electrical and electronics firms have increased the range of output in this industry. And there are miscellaneous new areas of production such as excavation equipment.

A striking fact is that 70 per cent of the new firms set up between 1959 and 1964 had foreign participation. These foreign firms accounted for 85 per cent of new investment resulting from the formation of new business concerns, and 77 per cent of new employment during this period. Production by these firms is for the export market and they thereby qualify for tax relief on profits and other subsidies. Most produce goods that are not highly expensive to transport, and many produce goods that are transported by air. While these firms concentrate upon exporting and have not become an integral part of the domestic economy, many foreign firms are using Irish personnel in managerial positions, as well as Irish factory workers.

SERVICE SECTOR

The service sector covers the part of employment and gross domestic product arising outside of agriculture, forestry, fishing, and industry. In 1960 roughly 45 per cent of the labor force was employed in this inclusive sector. In 1963 the service sector accounted for 42 per cent of national income as compared to 21 per cent for agriculture and 31 per cent for industry.

Over 90 per cent of the retail establishments are owned by individuals or partnerships, and there is one retail shop to every 70 people in the state. Modern self-service stores and supermarkets have increased in recent years, but for the most part retail trade remains a small business sector. The same can be said for wholesale businesses, although statistics on employee-employer ratios would indicate the wholesale trade has larger units, and more public firms than retail trade.

The professions are providing increased employment, particularly in health and education. However, there may be disguised underemployment in this group. In fact, the same statement can be made for retail and wholesale trades. Ireland has a ratio of employment in the service area comparable to that of more industrialized countries. There is room for cutting costs and increasing efficiency in many groups of this sector, and this would involve culling out the underemployed. As the economy industrializes, and as trade is freed and managerial abilities improve, it can be expected that competitive pressures will force increased efficiency. For these reasons, the employment forecast of the Second Program which foresees the service sector as providing large increases in employment opportunities does not appear realistic. While there is some room for expansion of the sector, its importance in respect to contributions to GNP and employment is already relatively high. Thus, the services cannot be expected to show employment increases comparable to those experienced in the history of many developed countries as they became more highly industrialized.

PUBLIC SECTOR

The public sector of Ireland has been quite active in the past in the area of agriculture and services as well as industry, and with the beginning of programming stepped forward to expand industrial output over existing levels (see Chapter 4). In recent years the state has financed approximately half of new domestic fixed capital formation. Current government expenditures ran between 20 per cent and 22 per cent of GNP between 1957/58 and 1962/63.

Ireland is a step ahead of most underdeveloped countries in the degree of development of her infrastructure, although she may be a step or a half step behind the more advanced industrial countries. Despite the fact that in the pre-planning days Ireland had invested in power, transport facilities, public services, houses, hospitals, and other infrastructure on a scale that was reasonably adequate by western European standards, industrial development and increases in national output were not forthcoming. The First Program for Economic Expansion, a five-year program begun in 1958, changed the emphasis of public investment from social areas such as housing to directly productive areas such as electricity, communications, and steel production, and channeled public funds into private investment, through credit and grants, in an effort to increase industrial activity. Actual public investment exceeded anticipated investment over the period of the First Program, helped along by the availability of funds with the rise in GNP of over 4 per cent per year. The fact that Ireland's programming efforts have been blessed by a relative abundance of capital is another point of divergence from most underdeveloped countries.

The budget in Ireland is divided into a current and a capital budget. The capital budget covers all capital expenditures of government departments, state-sponsored organizations (government enterprises, development corporations, etc.) and local authorities, and also includes agricultural and industrial credit. Deficits in the current budget are handled by borrowing, and surpluses are used to reduce the need for borrowing funds for long-term use. The budget is not used as an anti-cyclical device in Ireland, although the capital budget has been used as a vehicle for encouraging long-run growth.

Current budget expenditures increased at an increasing rate from £ 104.7 million in 1953/54 to approximately £ 180.6 million in 1963/64. Over this period there was a surplus in the current budget in the fiscal years 1958/59 and 1959/60; deficits were experienced in all other years. There has been no marked increase in deficits since planning began. The current budget had an average annual deficit of £ 3.3 million for the five years 1953/54 through

1957/58; for the five years from 1959/60 through 1963/64 the average annual deficit was £ 2.7 million.

The capital budget has risen at a steady pace since planning began from £ 38 million in 1958/59 to an estimated £ 80 million for 1963/64. Government capital expenditures are discussed in more detail in succeeding chapters. The rise in current and capital expenditures by the government over this period was not accompanied by any marked inflationary tendencies. There have been efforts in recent years to make taxes more indirect in order to encourage enterprise and discourage consumption. However, the expected rise in incomes, and hence taxes, forecast for 1970 would increase the proportion of taxes originating from income taxes to 34 per cent, above the rate of 25 per cent occurring in 1958/59. With the forecast increase, income taxes as a percentage of GNP would be at the rate of 9 per cent in 1970, as compared to 7.4 per cent in 1963. The main source of tax intake, taxes on expenditures, accounted for 73 per cent of tax income in 1958/59.

Central monetary policy cannot be used to influence the economy since the Irish monetary system is so interwoven with the British system as to preclude aggressive independent action. Irish money duplicates English money, and has the same exchange rate in international exchange markets. To some extent the absence of a shortage of funds in her capital markets may have been attributable to the inflow of funds from Britain attracted by the recent prosperous conditions in Ireland, and possibly fleeing England in anticipation of the 1964 Labor Party victory.

FOREIGN TRADE SECTOR

Exports and imports run roughly 40 per cent of GNP. Ireland has few natural resources other than grass. She has tended to specialize in livestock production for export in view of the absolute advantage she has in this area, and to import manufactured goods and raw materials.

As can be seen from Figure 1, there have been dramatic changes in Ireland's exports since 1952. At that time, over 80 per cent of foreign exchange earnings came from live animals, and food, drink, and tobacco, as compared to somewhat over 63 per cent in 1963. The change in these sectors as a percentage of total export trade was mainly the result of the dramatic increase in manufactured goods exports which composed only 6 per cent of exports in 1952, but rose to 22 per cent in 1963.

The history of changes in export earnings from 1952 to 1963 shows erratic movements in live animals and food, drink, and tobacco, while raw materials, a relatively small export class composed mainly of wool and hide products, fluctuated little. Most noteworthy was the sharp drop in food, drink, and tobacco earnings from almost £ 60 million in 1952/53 to about £ 33 million in 1955/56. This group remained below £ 50 million until 1960. Live animals

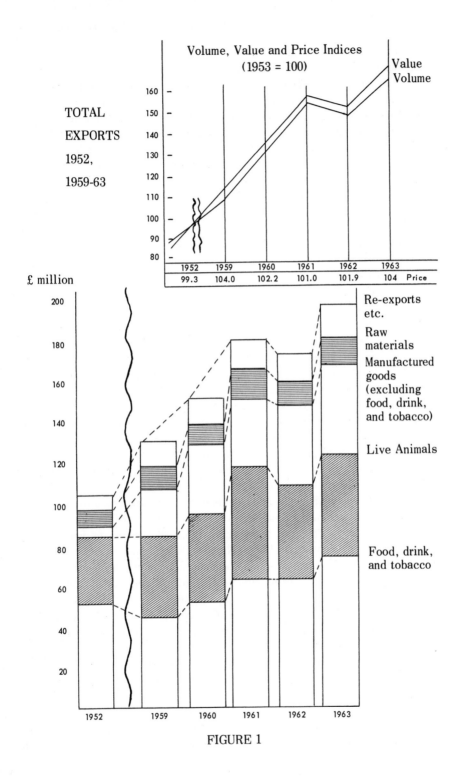

FIGURE 1

show a history of fluctuations of as much as £ 13 million from one year to the next, but have not dipped below their 1952/53 low during this period as food, drink, and tobacco did. While some of the movements in live animals and food, drink, and tobacco earnings have been a result of changes in terms of trade, there have also been changes in volume as demand conditions changed.

Exports of manufactured goods showed a slow ascent between 1952 and 1958 from £ 6 million to £ 17 million. From 1958 to 1959 they rose by almost as much as they had the previous six years, and continued to rise markedly, although somewhat less rapidly thereafter. Increases in manufactured goods have not suffered from adverse movements in the terms of trade as non-manufactured goods have.

Principal food and drink exports are frozen beef, stout and beer, fresh and chilled beef, bacon, chocolate crumb, creamery butter, mutton and lamb, vegetables, pork, and dried milk. Cattle make up roughly 80 per cent of live animal exports.

From 1952 until the sharp upswing in manufactured goods in 1958, the small amount of manufactured goods exports was concentrated in the areas of leather products, clothing, textiles, carpets, paper and paperboard products, rope and jute products, light machinery, printed matter, and glassware. In 1963 the old categories were still represented, and had increased in range of goods and foreign exchange earnings. Machinery increased dramatically, particularly exports of sewing machines, electrical equipment for the home, and electrical machinery. Metal and hardware instruments showed gains from very small representation in 1952 to substantial contributions to exports in 1963. Cement was added to the list of important exports along with pharmaceutical and medical products, plaster board, tires and tubes, furniture, and antiques. Petroleum products, a new export, made very noteworthy contributions to the value of exports in 1963.

Although the change in export markets has not been as striking as the sharp rise in manufactured goods exports since 1958, there has been a steady erosion of Britain's dominant position. In 1952, 86 per cent by value of exports from Ireland went to the United Kingdom, 6 per cent to the six European Economic Community countries, somewhat over 3 per cent to North America, and the remainder to scattered markets. In 1961, 74 per cent by pound value of exports went to the United Kingdom, 8 per cent to the United States, and 6 per cent to the European Economic Community. In 1963, 71 per cent of exports were sold in markets in the United Kingdom, 7.6 per cent to the European Economic Community, and 8.6 per cent to North America.

One reason for the concentration of exports to the United Kingdom market is that trade agreements between Ireland and Britain allow duty free access to the United Kingdom market for a large majority of Irish goods. After the United Kingdom and the United States, Germany is Ireland's largest trading partner, supplying an average 3.8 per cent of Ireland's imports during 1958-60, and taking 2.3 per cent of her exports. A factor affecting Ireland's trade with the European Economic Community is the common external tariff of the Community.

American purchases of Irish exports are heavily concentrated in the food, drink, and tobacco category, while roughly three-fourths of the United Kingdom's imports from Ireland were live animals, and food, drink, and tobacco in 1963. Countries other than the United Kingdom and North America purchased more Irish manufactured goods as a percentage of total imports from Ireland in 1963 than did Britain or America. About 73 per cent of Irish manufactured goods went to the United Kingdom in 1963, as compared to approximately 80 per cent in 1952. The European Economic Community, North America, and other areas as a group bought about equal quantities of Irish manufactured goods in 1963. The growth of Ireland's industrial sector may very well bring about a further drop in dependence upon Britain as an export market.

Ireland does not rely upon the United Kingdom market for imports to the degree she does for exports, but tends to run a surplus on trade account with the United Kingdom and a deficit with the European Economic Community. During the period 1961-63 imports from the United Kingdom averaged around 50 per cent of total imports, and imports from the United States equaled exports. Many raw materials and some semi-processed materials are imported for production purposes, including petroleum, chemicals, vehicles, and textile fibers. Machinery dominates the list of final goods, and has shown an upward trend with the industrialization of the economy. In the past, consumer goods have been severely limited by quotas and tariffs, and are still relatively limited.

The trade sector is vital to Ireland's expansion since she must have raw materials and machinery produced abroad. So far, foreign exchange shortages have not hobbled her development endeavor. Prior to 1957 the Central Bank was required by law to hold full external coverage for the currency. Thus Ireland began planning with a cache of foreign investments far in excess of her needs for working reserve balances. Moreover, reserves of the commercial banks, and even the resources of the government's general fund, have been invested abroad in marketable securities because of the scarcity of suitable domestic outlets for reserves. The increase in foreign investment in Ireland since 1958 has been another source of foreign exchange. Ireland's credit rating with international lending institutions is good, and she has been assured of access to borrowings in the future should she need further additions to foreign exchange in the carrying out of her industrialization program.

Another reason the export sector is considered by the Irish to be a crucial area in the endeavor to industrialize is because the home market has appeared to be saturated, and its expansion limited in the immediate short-run period by low incomes, a small population, and concentration of that population in the dependent age groups. The two programs for expansion state that industrialization depends upon export markets, both as outlets for the products of new industry, and as a means of expansion for established industries, some of which have not been able to achieve economies of scale because of a limited domestic market.

Once the strategy was adopted to make increased exports a keystone in the industrial efforts, there may have been a tendency not to give Say's law all the weight it should be accorded as a force contributing to enlarged domestic markets. An increase in incomes as output increases can result in levels of aggregate demand conducive to expansion of production for the home market. The continued emphasis upon exports in the Second Program, to the extent that it stems from a concern over a saturated home market rather than the need to finance raw material and other imports, may be reflective of the initial conservative estimate under the First Program of a 2 per cent per annum growth rate in GNP. There is a tendency for facets of development strategy, once devised, to escape re-examination with changing events; and ideas such as "saturated home market" can become a perpetuated phrase of exposition which may almost subconsciously guide actions after it is no longer applicable. Actually, the type of planning adapted in Ireland has been extolled by the French as highly conducive to bringing about increased incomes, demand, and output within a country through concerted action by all sectors in line with a feasible investment pattern of plan targets.

STATISTICAL PROFILE[7]

National income[8] at current prices increased over the period 1953-62 by 46 per cent, and by 58 per cent over the period 1953-63. Most of the increase was achieved after 1958, the year planning was inaugurated (see Table 1). Because of the decline in population as a result of emigration—mainly among the unemployed—the increase in national income per head during the period 1953-62 was 52 per cent. From 1953 to 1957, national income increased at the average annual rate in current prices of 1.7 per cent, whereas the change in national income from 1958 to 1962 was at the average annual rate of 8.1 per cent. In constant prices the growth in national income averaged 3.6 per cent from 1958 to 1962.

The increase in gross national product per head at constant prices was 23½ per cent between 1953 and 1962, that of total gross national product, 18½ per cent. Between 1953 and 1957 the real gross national product increased at an average annual rate of .7 per cent, and actually declined in 1958. In 1959, with the effects of planning reflected, there was a substantial increase of 4.4 per cent, and a continued rise at this average rate annually thereafter through 1964.

The following table listing the distribution of national income by sectors shows the decline in agricultural income as compared to non-agricultural income. While down in percentage terms, income originating in the agricultural sector increased from £ 126.7 million at market prices in 1953 to £ 145 million at market prices in 1962, or an increase of £ 18.3 million. The number employed

TABLE 1

NATIONAL INCOME AND GROSS NATIONAL PRODUCT

Year	National income	plus Provision for depreciation	plus Taxes on expenditure less subsidies	Gross national product at current market prices	Gross national product at 1953 market prices	Index of gross national product at constant market prices
			£ million			1953=100
1953	438.9	21.8	64.9	525.6	525.6	100.0
1954	440.9	23.7	64.1	528.7	531.2	101.1
1955	459.9	25.2	66.4	551.5	541.1	102.9
1956	455.5	29.7	74.1	559.3	535.6	101.9
1957	469.5	31.9	79.3	580.7	540.6	102.9
1958	482.1	33.0	83.4	598.5	524.9	99.9
1959	512.9	35.6	87.2	635.7	548.9	104.4
1960	547.4	37.9	86.1	671.4	579.7	110.3
1961	591.1	40.6	86.3	718.0	607.7	115.6
1962	640	43	91	774	623	118.5
1963	672	52	104	828	— —	— — —

Sources: Central Statistics Office, *National Income and Expenditure 1962*, Dublin: Stationery Office, 1963, p. 2, and
Statistical Abstract of Ireland, 1964, Dublin: Stationery Office, 1964, p. 272

TABLE 2

PERCENTAGE DISTRIBUTION OF NATIONAL INCOME BY SECTORS OF ORIGIN

Sector	1953	1954	1955	1956	1957	1958	1959	1960	1961	1962
					per cent					
Agriculture	29.1	27.0	28.2	25.7	27.4	24.9	25.4	24.3	23.6	22.5
Industry	26.2	27.4	26.8	27.6	26.0	27.1	27.4	28.2	29.0	30.0
Distribution, transport and communication	15.0	15.4	15.2	15.5	15.0	15.3	15.5	15.7	16.0	16.3
Other domestic	17.4	17.8	18.1	19.2	19.2	20.2	20.1	20.2	20.0	20.2
Public administration and defense	5.7	5.6	5.5	5.8	5.6	5.7	5.4	5.4	5.3	5.3
Emigrants' remittances	2.5	2.5	2.4	2.4	2.5	2.5	2.4	2.4	2.3	2.0
Other foreign income	4.1	4.3	3.8	3.8	4.2	4.2	3.8	3.8	3.8	3.7
Total national income	100.-	100.-	100.-	100.-	100.-	100.-	100.-	100.-	100.-	100.-

Source: Central Statistics Office, *National Income and Expenditure 1962*, Dublin: Stationery Office, 1963, p. 8.

in agriculture decreased from approximately 40 per cent of the labor force in 1956 to approximately 34 per cent in 1963.

Industry is the fastest growing sector in the economy. The only other sector to show a noteworthy growth rate is "other domestic," which includes actual and imputed income from hotels, restaurants, dwellings, banking and finance, and other personal service industries, including professional services. The increase in the industrial sector was from £ 114.3 million in 1953 to £ 193 million in 1962, a total increase of £ 78.3 million, over half (£ 38.2 million) of which was achieved from 1960 to 1962. Total income originating in the non-agricultural domestic sectors, taken before adjustment for stock appreciation, increased from £ 281 million at current prices in 1953 to £ 462 million in 1962, or by £ 181 million.

Employment in industry increased from approximately 16 per cent of the employed labor force in 1957 to approximately 18 per cent in 1963. Ireland is looking to industrial activity to help her export position and raise her level of income, but not to solve completely her unemployment problem, which has involved rates of postwar unemployment up to 10.6 per cent, not counting underemployment on the land. An encouraging note, however, is the fact that estimates for 1964 show unemployment to be down to 5.7 per cent of the labor force.

Personal expenditures on consumers' goods and services were 73 per cent of gross national product in 1953 and have stayed at that rate except for the years 1955-57, when they averaged approximately 75 per cent. Current government consumption runs at a fairly constant rate of close to 12 per cent of gross national product. While Ireland has inaugurated policies to try to keep consumption within limits and encourage saving, capital has not been a pivotal scarcity hobbling her expansion efforts. She has been able to attract foreign capital at a not inconsiderable rate, and by the end of 1963, her saving rate was 18 per cent of gross national product. A breakdown of the 18 per cent shows 2.7 per cent was external capital, 5.5 per cent business saving in the form of depreciation, and 9.8 per cent is termed "current saving," which includes saving of public and private companies, public authorities, and personal saving.[9]

A history of business and personal saving from 1955 to 1963 shows a marked increase in business saving after 1959, reflecting increased business profits, and a less dramatic increase in personal savings, which have tended to fluctuate more than business savings. Saving by public authorities makes up a very small portion of total saving. Over the 5 years 1959-63 "current savings" averaged 9.5 per cent of GNP as compared to 8.3 per cent over the years 1953-58.[10] This is not far from the 1960 savings rate of the United Kingdom (10.5 per cent), Belgium (10.6 per cent), or France (11.1 per cent), but is quite divergent from the 1960 rates in Western Germany (19.6 per cent), Italy (15.5 per cent), and the Netherlands, (20.9 per cent).[11]

Gross domestic physical capital formation fluctuated during the period

1953-62, ranging from a high of 18.3 per cent of GNP in 1955 to a low of 12 per cent in 1958; the year 1953 showed a capital formation figure of 16.6 per cent of GNP, which was not topped, with the exception of 1955, until 1962, when 16.8 per cent of GNP was devoted to gross domestic capital formation. Again, these investment rates are rather close to investment rates in the United Kingdom, Belgium, and France, but below the rates in Western Germany, Italy, and the Netherlands. [12] Much of Ireland's investment in the past has been in the areas of agriculture and dwellings. Their proportion of the total has been declining, however, since planning. In the years 1953-56, building and reconstruction of dwellings accounted for nearly one-fifth of gross domestic capital formation, but has amounted to only about one-seventh to one-ninth of the total since the government channeled public investment into more directly productive areas.

Ireland experienced more inflationary pressures in the five years prior to 1958 than she did in the five years of expansion after 1958. Between 1953 and 1958 prices increased 16.5 per cent, or 3.3 per cent per year on the average. From 1958 to 1963 prices rose 11.9 per cent, or at an average rate of about 2.4 per cent per year. These facts are welcomed in a country such as Ireland where traditional practice is to avoid inflation because of its ramifications upon international trade. However, 1964 and 1965 showed increasing rates of inflation—over 6 per cent in 1964—following continued expansion and wage increases above productivity gains. The government has initiated a series of measures to try to dampen the inflationary trend. Because of the high dependence upon Britain's market, Ireland will not suffer a great deal from a rate of inflation that does not exceed Britain's rate of price increases.

Prior to the changes that came after 1959, Ireland's pattern of external trade possessed two well-defined characteristics. Her exports were largely (75 per cent) agricultural products, and concentrated upon the United Kingdom market; and there was consistently a substantial deficit in her balance of visible trade, with visible exports paying for only about 60 per cent of imports. The largest single source of non-visible earnings was tourism, which made up on the average one-third of total net invisible exports between 1953 and 1957. [13] The following table shows export and import changes in pounds and in percentages from 1953 to 1963, and the balance of trade for this period.

Ireland's expansion efforts were helped by the favorable demand conditions in external markets between 1958 and 1964. Should the generally prosperous conditions among European Free Trade Association and European Economic Community countries change, and Britain fail to solve her trade problems in the near future, Ireland's expansion efforts may be adversely affected.

Inasmuch as Ireland's development goals involve importation of raw materials and machinery, an increase of 50 per cent in GNP during the decade 1960 to 1970 and increased levels of employment are dependent upon the expansion of the export sector. Exports of goods and services—agricultural and

TABLE 3

FOREIGN TRADE 1953-63

(£ million) 1953=100

	1953	1954	1955	1956	1957	1958	1959	1960	1961	1962	1963
Exports of Goods and Services											
£	198	197	197	195	217	221	230	255	293	294	320
	100	100.4	97.6	97.3	106.4	104.4	105.8	118.9	136.5	133.7	--
Imports of Goods and Services											
£	205	203	233	209	208	222	238	256	292	307	342
	100	98.2	109.1	95.9	90.7	100	109.3	115.4	130.1	136.5	--
Balance of Trade											
£	-7	-6	-36	-14	+9	-1	-8	-1	+1	-13	-22

Sources: Central Statistics Office, *National Income and Expenditure 1962*, Dublin: Stationery Office, 1963, p. 36 and p. 13, and *Statistical Abstract of Ireland 1964*, Dublin: Stationery Office, 1964, p. 274.

industrial goods, tourism, etc.—must increase by 75 per cent in order for the 1970 target to be achieved. Agriculture exports are vulnerable to world market conditions and limitations on demand. The burden of goal achievement will thus be borne by industrial exports which must increase by over 150 per cent during the decade to assure program success. The Second Program plans on a continuation of the trend in the export sector initiated by the large spurt in foreign investment begun in the 1950's. A stable political condition, developed infrastructure, and surplus of labor have been factors working in Ireland's favor in the attraction of foreign investors, especially investors from Europe where there has been a shortage of labor for the past five years. The tendency for industrial exports to diversify Ireland's export markets means that duty-free access to the United Kingdom market may not play as strategic a part in the future as it has played in the past, especially if Britain and Ireland enter the European Economic Community.

SUMMARY

Ireland can be characterized as a nation in transition. Since 1958 she has been moving toward a more highly industrialized economy, and away from an economy primarily dependent upon agriculture which suffered in the past from stagnation, low incomes, unemployment, and high emigration rates. The government adopted two programs for economic expansion to increase the industrial content of the economy, and thereby raise income levels, reduce unemployment, and stem the high levels of out-migration.

A limited range of protected industries, often composed of relatively small, internally held firms, supplied the small home market in the past. Industry in Ireland is highly dependent upon imported raw materials since there are few natural resources other than agricultural resources. Expanded industrial activity since 1958 has been mainly concentrated in the export field, and has broadened the industrial base and industrial export markets. Ireland is still dependent upon the United Kingdom market for 70 per cent of her export sales, but the growth of industrial exports has lessened this dependence as compared to the period when farm products completely dominated the export industry.

Perhaps Ireland's pivotal scarcity is in the area of managerial and entrepreneurial ability. She also faces problems in the areas of marketing access and know-how in international markets, technological advancements in products and processes of production, and procurement of raw materials, including sources of energy. Ireland is attempting to overcome these scarcities in several ways, one of the more important being the attraction of foreign capital and managerial ability to her shores. A stable democracy, surplus of labor, and developed infrastructure have worked in Ireland's favor in this respect. Ireland's duty-free access and proximity to the United Kingdom market, as well as her nearness to the continent, have been capitalized upon in attracting manufacturers that have relatively low transportation costs and/or can transport by air. Government action in the areas of direct investment, the creation of a growth perspective, and the provision of inducements for private investment, is playing a large role in Ireland's development efforts. Democratic support for this action has sprung from the alarm of the nation over its declining population, and Britain's proposed entry into the European Economic Community, an eventuality which would affect Ireland's favored trade position with the United Kingdom, her dominant export market.

Notes

1. *Time Magazine,* July 12, 1963, p. 37.

2. These figures are derived from OEEC statistics and quoted in *Economic Development,* Dublin: Stationery Office, 1958, p. 10. Figures by Colin Clark in *The Conditions of Economic Progress* (3rd ed.), London: MacMillan and Company, Limited, 1957, pp. 153-154, given in "international units" place Ireland's real income per head in 1951 at 431 IU's. The 1951 real income per head expressed in IU's for other countries were: Denmark 618, France 509, Great Britain 597, Greece 181, Italy 250, Japan 210, Netherlands 506, Brazil 182 and United States 1,122. In a study showing 1955 per capita gross national product and ranking among western European countries (J. Walter Thompson Company, *The Western European Markets,* New York: McGraw-Hill Company, Inc., 1957, p. 11) Ireland is ranked 14th out of 20 European countries, above Italy ($450) and behind Austria ($545), with a 1955 per capita GNP of $481, as compared to that of the United Kingdom, $1,046, France $1,100, Denmark $924, Greece $263, Netherlands $716, Western Germany $780, and Spain $318.

3. Statistics for this section are taken mainly from David O'Mahony, *The Irish Economy,* Cork: Cork University Press, 1964.

4. *Ibid.,* p. 14.

5. *Economic Development,* Dublin: Stationery Office, 1958, p. 13.

6. "By tradition, due mostly to the historical circumstances which deprived us of the benefits—and perhaps on the other hand, fortunately of the evils—of the Industrial Revolution of the last century, parents heretofore decided that the bright ones of the family should be sent on for the professions while the mediocre should go into business." *Industrial Review* (Journal of Federation of Irish Industries), March-April, 1964, 5.

7. Except when otherwise indicated, data for this section came from the Central Statistics Office, Dublin. The main source is *National Income and Expenditure 1962,* Dublin: Stationery Office, 1963.

    8. National income statistics given here are according to official United Nations definitions.

    9. *Second Program for Economic Expansion,* Part II, Dublin: Stationery Office, 1964, p. 287.

    10. *Ibid., p.* 288.

    11. *Second Program for Economic Expansion,* Part I, Dublin: Stationery Office, 1963, p. 55

    12. *Ibid.,* p. 49.

    13. *Op. cit., Economic Development,* pp. 14-15.

FRENCH INFLUENCE ON IRISH PLANNING

Ireland is perhaps a living refutation of the suspicion that only the Gallic mind could comprehend and carry out the accusedly quixotic product of economic philosophy called French planning. Finding in this concept of planning the relatively illusive but important aspects of economic expansion, and deriving virtues from its very nebulousness, the Irish have been able to capture the spirit of the Gallic offspring. They like to say they are "only creating a big fuss." While there is a more tangible aspect to their planning than this, the Irish are undoubtedly counteracting seemingly inbuilt pessimism and inertia with their "big fuss." In fact, the French concept of planning has many facets that render it highly applicable to the Irish scene, including publicizing progress.

What is the "spirit of the plan" whose illusiveness confounds, but whose role demands attention? First of all, the spirit of the plan is to be found in recognition of the benefits of getting together to exchange information, and the virtues of discussion between the public and private sectors.[1] To the extent that available information is disseminated and used, and additional information sought and recorded, uncertainty is reduced, and the action that results has a greater chance of being rational and successful.

The "spirit of the plan" is also to be found in the lightness of structure of the planning machinery, and the setting of non-compulsory targets, usually on an industry level, through the joint consultation of industry and government. It involves the ideas that concerted action has readily acknowledgeable benefits once these actions are considered and discussed by the groups involved in the results, and that participant planning, bolstered by indirect incentives and government initiative, will result in the supporting and carrying out of plan goals to a large degree.

This does not mean the French type of planning is merely indicative. It is what the French call "reasonably voluntary," by which they mean that the plan is "active" in the sense that the choice of production targets not only changes the producers' anticipations, but also constitutes a commitment for State action—usually in the form of economic constraints in preference to administrative constraints.[2] This ability to ameliorate constraint is in no sense a small contribution to the theory of planning. In fact the French have referred to it as a striking innovation: "The chief original feature of French planning is that it deliberately rejects absolute constraint for the realization of the Plan, while being concerned with seeing that its realization is assured in a suitable manner."[3]

Herein is contained the idea that the manner in which the plan is drawn up can help to bring about its fulfillment. Co-operation, nurtured and coddled by a government which provides a growth perspective, can eliminate the need for government control to a large extent. Thus, Premier Georges Pompidou, in presenting the Fourth Plan to the National Assembly, referred to it as "a little like the Kantian ethic: a text without obligation or penalty."

Just how concrete or influential is such a plan? The long-term French plans are an attempt to trace the optimum possible course of development, rather than set out detailed policy blueprints. Writing of the French plans, Wellisz states:

> The plans—explicitly or implicitly—carry policy recommendations, but actual economic policy is molded by short-term considerations and is often strongly influenced by developments exogenous to the national economies. Nevertheless, the plans indicate broad policy goals, and the recommendations contained in the plans have an undeniable influence on short-term governmental decisions.[4]

French short-term plans are an official expression of governmental economic policy that has emphasized resource allocation among types of consumer goods, regions of the country, etc. Consumer industries are relatively free to make their own decisions, but the pattern of investment is strongly modified by the intricate French system of differential taxes, subsidies, and credit controls. The plan is followed quite closely in the socialized sector. Wellisz writes:

> Since the government provides about one-third of all investment funds in France and controls another 40 per cent, its financial control is quite powerful. Thus in practice most of the heavy industries (especially steel) follow the plan quite closely....[5]

In fact, it was the nationalized industries that set the pace in the early years (1950's) of French planning, showing a sluggish and timid private sector what a little boldness could accomplish. As a result, at least one author concludes that state firms, by helping to push the economy toward the full utilization of resources, and through the rationalization of production, may have added to rather than subtracted from the creation of capacity in private industry in the 1950's.[6]

The Irish have borrowed and adapted this concept of planning which delimits planning as a system of coordinated guidance, and which is very reminiscent of the old Physiocratic idea of the government as orchestra leader, seeing that everyone is in tune, and harmonizing what might otherwise be discordant independent action. The looseness and democratic nature of this system of planning fits Ireland's needs admirably.

ADAPTATION OF FRENCH PLANNING TO THE IRISH ECONOMY

A country faced with the magnitude of the task of trying to transform its economy within a limited time period from one highly dependent upon agriculture to one with a large industrialized sector could be drawn to a more rigid planning network of a less voluntary nature than the French style of planning. In fact, however, a less voluntary type of planning would be neither admired nor needed in Ireland, given the strategy she has decided to use in the development process, and the particular circumstances of the Irish economy, including the external influences upon it. As will be seen more fully in the next chapter, the indirect controls and methods for implementing the Irish expansion programs in large part supplant the need for large administrative constraints, and the over-fullfillment of the goals of the First Program for Economic Expansion has precluded any consideration of the need for more rigid planning controls.

What are the particular strategies and circumstances that have led Ireland to embrace the French planning concepts and adapt them to her economy? First it should be mentioned that the philosophy and institutional machinery set up to carry out plan goals under the French type of planning are compatible with democratic institutions and avoid threatening democratic values. Ireland's political sophistication, literacy rate, democratic institutions, and attachment to private property and free enterprise undoubtedly influenced her choice of planning techniques. What is more, these characteristics enabled her to reject a more centralized type of planning; for, as Gunnar Myrdal points out, it is in the underdeveloped countries with weak political and administrative apparatuses and largely illiterate populations that "a sort of super-planning" has to be staged.[7] Thus, democratic institutions developed prior to the advent of planning have helped in the choosing of a type of program that will pose little if any threat to those institutions. If the French variety of planning had not worked so well as it has, Ireland might have been faced with the problem of weighing the detrimental political effects of stronger planning constraints in order to build herself up as a nation, against the changes such planning techniques might require in accustomed democratic procedures. So far, she has not had to weigh these alternatives.

What has been called "creating a fuss" might also be termed "creating a growth perspective." For years Ireland has channeled some of her most talented individuals into government service. It was not unnatural that the government would create the drive and leadership in reversing the dreariness of repetitive stagnation which the economy had experienced in the past. The French type of planning provided an admirable framework for poking and nudging the dormant private sector into self appraisal, and for setting up institutions through which the growth perspective could permeate the society and instill the idea of progress into a people steeped in pessimism since the days of the potato famine. The government alarmed a nation faced with de-population through emigration, thus drawing upon the forces of nationalism to support the expansion endeavor. Ireland had to be convinced not only that something had to be done, but that something could be done.

Large benefits have been reaped from the setting up of programs to accumulate information necessary to long-run and short-run forecasts and rational economic action at the firm, industry, and national level. The government has led the way in this, and endeavored to educate the private firms on the benefits of long-range forecasting, capital planning, rationalization of production, and the gathering of information upon which to base sound decisions in these spheres. Because of a distrust of competitors, trade organizations such as exist in the United States are largely non-existent and the government has had to instigate and supplement the gathering of industrial statistics. Adaptation Councils have been set up at the urging of the government to encourage group discussion of problems involved in the freeing of trade and the promotion of exports. And at the government's instigation, Committees on Industrial Organization were set up for all major industrial sectors in Ireland. Even the Federation of Irish Industries is headed by a former civil servant who is steeped in the philosophy and goals of the planning programs, and is creating a spirit of cooperation within the association.

PLAN GOALS AND STRATEGIES

As in the case of French planning, Irish planning has involved the out-lining of consistent goals and deciding among alternative uses for limited government funds within the framework of a growth plan.[8] Early French planning, as described by M. Claude Gruson, Director-General, French National Institute of Statistics and Economic Studies, bears striking resemblance to the Irish situation. M. Gruson writes:

> At that moment (1949), the facts of having explicitly fixed growth objectives and of having conceived the great basic programs, especially those of the nationalized industries, so as to make the basic programs compatible with the growth objectives, did indeed play a great part in the psychological reactions of an economy which...did not know before the war even what the idea of economic growth

meant. But at that time the objectives of growth could be formulated very simply. The living standard of the French was still relatively low. Consumption and investment could still set their sights on objectives that, in detail, could rather easily be defined intuitively. Under these conditions it was sufficient, as experience has shown, to formulate in a global way, a growth target, and to take a certain number of fundamental decisions leading towards that target, in order, without great difficulty, to set the whole mechanism going.[9]

In circumstances similar in many ways to those of France after the war, the Irish have "intuitively" isolated their pivotal scarcities—one of the most important being that of the absence of managerial ability—and devised a growth strategy. And similarly, an over-all growth target has been formulated for the Irish economy and the more obvious, basic steps have been taken toward the achievement of these goals.

In these formative years of planning the Irish economy has exhibited rather obvious shortcomings and needs in the light of newly formed goals, and the techniques and methodology of the planning process have remained rather loose-knit and flexible. For example, the procedure under the Second Program was as follows: Feasible plan goals were worked out by an iterative method, i.e., a trial and error method, sometimes termed a method of "successive approximations." The planning section of the Department of Finance looked first at the implications of several growth rates from the perspective of policy actions, external forces upon the economy, and availability of resources, elaborating in more detail those rates that seemed feasible. These elaborations started with a simple breakdown of the economy into, for example, output or expenditure, and proceeded by successive approximations based upon national income accounts to more detailed breakdowns that involved, among other things, making projections of employment, sectoral outputs, productivity by sectors, and elasticity of demand by sectors. A check was run on the selected growth rates considered for the Second Program by building a ten-sector input-output model of the Irish economy and using this model to check upon the consistency and feasibility of the growth rates calculated under the iterative method. From the two methods a growth rate of 4.14 per cent per annum emerged under the Second Program as the highest possible rate, given the limitations, economic and political, acting upon the economy.

In isolating pivotal scarcities and devising a growth strategy, Ireland started with a survey of the economy showing its potential and its shortcomings.[10] The prospect of a vanishing nation was imminent if the trend of the late fifties continued and net population increases were below net emigration levels. Agriculture presented no opportunity to provide employment for additions to the labor force. In fact, efficiency in agriculture demanded consolidation of small farms, more mechanization, and less workers on the farm. With the advent of the *Fianna Fail* party to power in the late 1950's, emphasis was given to the need for the economy to industrialize in order to provide higher living standards for the people and provide jobs to stem the flow of emigrants.

Not only was the goal of industrialization endorsed, but the need to set a pace for industrialization became evident, given the sluggishness of the industrial sector. Moreover, near the close of the decade of the 1950's external pressures upon Ireland reinforced the need for timely action. The tariff walls raised in the thirties would have to fall, and with them, small, inefficient producers. Behind these walls Ireland had built up a cadre of industries catering predominantly to the small Irish market. But, economic benefits to be derived from protecting infant industries had long since been obtained, and actual experience had shown there was little linkage effect from protecting the latter stages of development; rather, a pyramid of protection grew up to insulate industries from foreign competition at all stages and resulted in inefficient production and proliferation of products produced by each firm.

The threat of European Economic Community entry provided the government with a stick which it could use in goading the private sector of the Irish economy into increased efficiency and consolidation of production lines. Despite the changed circumstances surrounding Ireland's possible future entry into the European Economic Community, the strategy of decreasing tariffs is being persistently followed, and the government is isolated from political reactions by its ability to cast blame for its actions upon the hard facts of life visited upon Ireland as a result of external conditions beyond the government's control. It should be mentioned that along with the stick, the government has used the carrot also; it has provided subsidies for adaptation expenditures and agencies for consultation and advice to ease the pains of transition.

It became apparent that the lowering of tariffs and encouragement of the private sector, even when combined with the use of the government sector to advance industrialization, would not produce enough new jobs, new investment, and, particularly, new exports fast enough to create the needed momentum to get the Irish economy into the "take-off" stage within a reasonable period of time. Once the possibilities of the home market were surveyed and found to be small, given the level of demand and incomes—even too small in many cases to realize technological and other economies of scale—the key to growth was seen to be in the increasing of exports. Only through exporting could Ireland hope to provide for increasing imports needed to expand industrial activity and raise living standards. Only through exporting could small firms catering to the home market enlarge their operations to the optimum output size. And only through exporting, given the limited home demand during the initial development stages, could enough new industrial activity be fomented to induce new employment opportunities in the goods and service sectors to stem the large-scale emigration.

At some point in her strategy decision-making Ireland took note of the advantages of and the need for foreign capital. Foreign capital could quicken the pace at which the country could develop above that of relying upon internal resources, thus providing more jobs for the economy and creating a momentum conducive to further expansion. Foreign capital could bring with it managerial abilities, a vitally scarce resource in Ireland, and could aid in the training of domestic managerial talent. Technological know-how would be imported and firms attracted with marketing channels established in the international trading markets, increasing the likelihood of a successful and immediate jump in exports. And foreign capital would decrease the necessity for stringent saving measures by the Irish people to finance their own industrial expansion.

As success could not be forecast in the attraction of foreign firms to Irish soil, this strategy was undoubtedly thrown into the hopper with the others in the early days of strategy formation. Measures were taken which would, hopefully, attract capital from other countries. The success of these measures is studied intensely in later chapters. It is only necessary to mention now that a large measure of the success of the planning program in Ireland is attributable to the influx of foreign firms that provided approximately 80 per cent of the new private investment during the first six years of programming. Herein is a feature of distinct contrast with French planning.

In devising planning strategies, Ireland had to consider the acceptability of the implementation methods which would accompany their application. Having accepted the philosophy of planning that sought to sidestep direct restraints, Ireland's goal-attainment methods were somewhat circumscribed, and her strategies necessarily reflected this circumscription. As John P. Lewis has pointed out:

> It is often convenient to speak as though the "planning" of policy and the administrative "implementation" of policy decisions are two distinctly different activities. Actually, however, they are both parts of the same decision-making continuum. Thus, anyone concerned to establish an effective central economic programing procedure must be vitally interested in the administrative arrangements that are available for translating the plans into action....[11]

Both programs have outlined the more important methods of achieving expansion, along with the program goals.

THE FIRST PROGRAM FOR ECONOMIC EXPANSION

The First Program for Economic Expansion was a fifty-page White Paper issued in November, 1958, designed to consolidate and orient government action behind a growth philosophy. Describing its First Program, the government wrote in Chapter 1 of the Second Program:

It outlined the objectives of economic policy in agriculture, industry, tourism and other main sectors of activity. It dealt specifically with the role of the state in promoting economic development, both direct- ly through state investment and indirectly through the encouragement of private enterprise by grants, loans, tax incentives and other means. The program was introduced at a time of concern about Ire- land's capacity to progress economically at the rate needed to give all who want to live in Ireland an acceptable income. Its aim was to accelerate progress by strengthening public confidence, indicating the opportunities for development, and encouraging a progressive, expansionist outlook. [12]

The First Program, as the Second, was issued at a politically opportune time. It stressed the need for an answer to the challenge of England's mem- bership application in the European Economic Community, and a positive outline for action by the state at a time when public social needs such as housing, hospitals and schools were satisfied to the extent that there would be a drop in government spending in future years if the state concerned itself only with continuing existing policies in regard to social needs. The govern- ment chose to redefine the objectives of state spending and acted by setting up a five-year plan to examine thoroughly, and plan in relation to, Ireland's pressing needs of the present and future years. These were the beginning years of Ireland's experiment with programming. The government provided a growth perspective, and it set about to provoke and induce private action, and install the institutions for a democratically congenial framework of con- certed action.

The first step of the strategy for development was to orient government programs toward "productive" expenditures within the over-all goal of in- dustrial expansion and to set up machinery for private sector participation in the future. In fact, the actual machinery for consultation with the private sector and participation in industry growth targets by the private sector was not in operation until after publication of the first part of the Second Program, one reason being that political strategy demanded publication of the Second Program before consultations were completed. Not surprisingly, then, the government concentrated in the First Program on "creating a big fuss" and channeling government action and thought into projects designed to provide Ireland with conditions for industrial growth. The First Program states:

Except to the extent to which it may be state-financed, the vital contribution which the private sector can make to economic progress is not expressly dealt with. The program is, however, based on the principle that, in the future as in the past the private sector will be the principal source of new productive projects. It is hoped that the publication of the program will act as a stimulus to industrialists in the formulation of the new projects and will be of assistance to them in the preparation of their production plans. [13]

Not foreseeing the large influx of foreign capital, and out of inherent Irish pessimism, the real growth rate of GNP was set under the First Program at 2 per cent per year. The over-all goals of the Program were twofold: first, to stem emigration through stimulating home employment opportunities in industry, and second, to prepare to compete in and join the European Economic Community through tariff reduction, and an expansion of industry in the export sector. The main aspects of the Program are summarized under "Agriculture," "Fisheries" and "Industry." The goals of these sectors were not broken down into target figures except for state industries. The goals and the means of carrying out these goals as set out in the First Program are listed below.

Agriculture

Agricultural objectives under the First Program are as follows:

1. A steady increase in agricultural output and exports based on increased productivity, which in turn will be fostered mainly by a policy of grassland improvement related to increased use of lime and phosphates in particular, and to the introduction of improved methods of management.

2. Eradication of bovine tuberculosis in the shortest possible period.

3. A considerable further development of agricultural education, advisory services and research (in association with *An Foras Taluntais*).

4. Improved agricultural marketing and the further development of trade relations with the countries where Irish agricultural products are marketed.

5. Application of state aid so as to secure expansion of output at lower unit cost, leading to competitive selling prices and, through higher turnover, to an increase in net agricultural incomes. A measure of price support will be maintained for wheat, beef, milk, and pigs.

Specific measures for carrying out the above goals include government action as follows:

1. Subsidization of price of fertilizer for five years.

2. Expansion of use of grass silage for winter feeding by farmers.

3. Financing of breeding research and leasing of top quality stock bulls to breeders.

4. Credit to farmers so that they can increase the number of cattle.

5. State aid to help finance research in areas of marketing, transport, and fuller utilization of by-products.

6. Reduction of the subsidy on butter exports now in low demand by breeding for meat. Investigation of possibilities for increasing exports of other milk products, supplying capital where conditions are good.

7. Improvement of pig breeding and reduction of subsidies.

8. Restriction of wheat crops to avoid surplus under guaranteed price program.

9. Encouragement of farmers to use more credit, to be supplied under the auspices of the state to achieve above goals.

Fisheries

Marine products are a natural resource that has not been fully developed. Demand is good and the Irish program lays plans for building up the industry. Plans include:

1. Setting up facilities for training fishermen, improving harbors.

2. Building of factories if private firms do not readily enter areas of fish processing, storage, and distribution.

3. Sponsoring survey of coasts and other research activity.

In marine products (seaweed processing, etc.) the government will participate in industrial production if existing firms fail to increase their output. The same approach will be applied to the forest industry.

Industry

Goals for industry are:

1. Stimulation of a "vast increase" in private industrial development, mainly for the export markets since home demand is not large and the small home market is fairly well supplied by home industry that has been protected for over twenty-five years by high tariffs.

2. Where possible, have manufacturing activities cover all processes from the basic raw material stage. (The small resource base and the past policy of import substitution fostered by tariff walls leave little area for expansion here.)

The means of carrying out the above goals are listed as:

1. Attraction of foreign capital through:

    a) Continuation of policy of permitting foreign industrial promoters to reside in Ireland, and the employment of foreign managers and technical experts in industrial enterprises.

    b) Continuation of policy contained in Industrial Development (Encouragement of External Investment) Act of 1958.

2. Provision of credit, underwriting of public issues, subscription to shares, and provision of hire-purchase facilities for acquisition of industrial plant and machinery, through the Industrial Credit Company, Limited, a state agency.

3. Cutting of tariffs.

4. Tax remission on export profits and on expenditure on mineral development, shipping, plant and machinery, new industrial buildings, etc.

5. Industrial research and state support of technical assistance schemes.

6. Establishment of *Coras Trachtala Teo* to promote exports and carry out market research.

7. The provision of grants through the state agency *An Foras Tionscal*.

8. Industrial promotion through the Industrial Development Authority.

9. Sponsoring of government projects where this can be justified for "reasons of public policy" or where "it is considered unlikely that they will be initiated by private interests."[14] State participation in industry under the plan includes:

    a) Encouragement of existing state bodies to extend their activities into "projects related to their main spheres of operation and to test the profitability of new lines and new markets."[15]

    b) Exploring further the possibility of a nitrogenous fertilizer factory.

    c) Modernization and expansion of the state steel works at Haulbowline, County Cork, to cost about £ 2 million.

10. Introduction of legislation to enable the state to make further contribution towards Irish Shipping Limited's development program, and to make provision for increased borrowing powers by the Company.

11. Subsidization of the railroad by writing off advances from the Exchequer and other measures to enable it to eliminate losses by March 31, 1964.

12. Expansion of electricity to meet potential needs up to 2,645 million units—as against actual demand in 1958 of 1,775 million—at a cost of £ 130 million.

13. Doubling of turf (peat) production by 1963. *Bord na Mona* (the state turf monopoly) will spend an estimated £ 21 million to achieve this target.

14. A twenty-five year tax exemption for industries in customs-free zone of Shannon Airport.

15. A new airport at Cork at initial capital cost of £ 1 million.

16. The provision of funds by the government for telephone capital development.

17. Legislation to assist mineral exploration and exploitation.

18. Continuation of encouragement of development of tourism, and the setting aside by government of one million pounds to assist, by way of grants, a ten-year program for the improvement of infrastructure and non-revenue earning development, which is part of a fully coordinated plan for a particular resort, substantially contributed to by local development groups.

19. Abolition of "restrictive practices."

The First Program, a five-year plan for coordinated coherence and orientation of action in the government sector, foresaw a 2 per cent annual growth in real GNP as feasible, based upon such government action as outlined. Over the period of the plan there was an increase in real GNP of more than 4 per cent per annum, mainly as a result of increased industrial production in the private sector—specifically the industrial export sector. From comparable base figures of contribution to gross output, agriculture increased at an annual average rate of 2.7 per cent during the First Program, as compared with a 7.2 per cent per annum average growth rate for industry. The service sector,[16] which has retained a relative share of national income of approximately 40 per cent over the past few years, grew at a rate slightly less than half the 7.2 per cent of the industrial sector.

The pace was set in the industrial sector by industrial exports which increased from an annual value of £ 32.8 million in 1958 to £ 62.2 million in 1963, i.e., by over 90 per cent. There were 133 new undertakings with foreign participation during the period of the First Program exporting almost 100 per cent of their output and representing a total capital investment of £ 38.5 million. In 1962 and 1963 the inflow of foreign capital was at the approximate rate of £ 20 million a year.

The dramatic increase in total industrial production of 42 per cent over the span of the first program (compared to an increase of about 24 per cent in real GNP) meant an increase in numbers at work in industry of 2.4 per cent per year. The number employed in services rose slightly during the First Program, so that the number at work in that sector in 1963 was approximately 39.7 per cent of the total labor force, while the number in agriculture fell to 22 per cent of total employment. For the first time since 1946 there was no decline in total laborers at work, and employment held steady.[17]

The rise in the volume of industrial production index for manufacturing was from 105.8 in 1958 (1953 = 100) to 151.9 in 1963; the rise for mining and manufacturing together from 106.5 in 1958 to 154.1 in 1963; and the industrial production index for all industries and services rose from 101.9 in 1958 (1953 = 100) to 134.5 in 1962. Index numbers for the volume of agricultural output show a rise from 94.6 in 1958 (1953 = 100) to 110.8 in 1962. [18] Unemployment as a percentage of the insured labor force fell from 8 per cent in 1958 to 5.5 per cent in the fourth quarter of 1963 (this includes persons waiting to emigrate). State capital expenditure rose during the period of the First Program from £ 37.89 million in 1958/59 to £ 78.50 million in 1963/64, which was 35 per cent higher than the estimate made for state expenditure at the time of the First Program in 1958. It is estimated that emigration has declined to the extent that there is no longer a net decline in population.

The progress was achieved without the addition of confiscatory taxes or high rates of inflation. The consumer price index stood at 116.5 (1953 = 100) in 1959, and rose to 128.4 in 1963. Total taxation in Ireland as a percentage of gross national product was 22.5 per cent in 1958/59, 22 per cent in 1960/61, and 23.7 per cent in 1963/64. Taxation rates are forecast as rising to 26.2 per cent of gross national product by 1970, a figure that still will leave Irish taxes below rates of any of the European Economic Community or European Free Trade Association countries except Switzerland and Portugal. When it was decided to reduce quotas, tariffs, and other barriers to trade in the late 1950's, a retail turnover tax was added to take up the slack in tax income that would result from lower customs and excise duties, which in the past provided around 50 per cent of tax intake. Taxes on expenditures in 1963 were 15.8 per cent of gross national product and income taxes were 7.4 per cent of gross national product. The Second Program anticipates that income taxes, which provided 25 per cent of government tax intake in 1958, will provide 34 per cent in 1970 as employment and incomes rise with increases in gross national product, and that taxes on expenditures will provide 64 per cent of government tax income in 1970, the remaining 2 per cent coming from taxes on capital.

It was not without considerable pride that the government pointed to the fact that Ireland had reached the final year (1963) of her first experience in planning a "much better-off nation than in 1958," [19] and in fact achieved "a greater rate of growth than was achieved during any similar period in the history of the State." [20] The success of the program stemmed from the activities of the government and industrial sectors, and particularly depended upon the unparalleled sharp rise in industrial exports as a result of the influx of foreign firms. For a nation depending upon foreign markets to the great extent that Ireland does, the propitious external circumstances existing throughout the First Program, including the spur to efficiency of the European Economic Community threat, also must be given credit. There was enough glory left over, however, to lend more than a modicum of credence to the government's boast that "These achievements demonstrate how effective a positive, integrated statement of attainable objectives, backed by state aids and incentives, can be."[21] And as the March, 1964, OECD *Survey on Ireland* noted regarding the First Program, "Not the least of its achievements was to convince public opinion in Ireland that more rapid economic growth was feasible."[22]

THE SECOND PROGRAM FOR ECONOMIC EXPANSION

Flushed from the success of the First Program, the government planned with new fervor and attention to detail in Parts I and II of the Second Program. Yet, despite the greatly expanded nature of the Second Program and the development in the methodology and machinery of planning, planning in Ireland is still a rather light, deliberately flexible framework designed to focus public and private efforts upon the problems of economic expansion. The strategy of the Second Program resembles that of the First Program in that it concentrates upon government action and inducements to a large degree. However, plan targets have now been devised for industrial groups and increased participation by the private sector is sought, particularly through the machinery set up for the review and revision of industry targets under the Second Program.

Comparing the First and Second Programs, it is noticeable that the more detailed and, necessarily, the more consistent the planning goals or targets, the more evident become certain projects that would be helpful to growth. Thus, in the Second Program Ireland is still in the stage of uncovering relatively obvious areas of needed action simply by examining carefully her educational policies, labor force movements, tax laws, economic performance, etc., from the perspective of her growth potential. Such an examination has resulted in the announced objective of an annual average growth in GNP of 4.2 per cent over the years 1964-70. The over-all objectives of the Program and the breakdowns by sectors, as modified in Part II of the Program issued in July, 1964, are listed below.

Over-all Objectives of the Second Program

1. Raise the real income of the community by 50 per cent in the 1960's in line with the collective target of the OECD, which will mean a 35 per cent increase in GNP from 1964 to 1970.

2. Assure the progressive reduction of involuntary emigration so that by 1970 net yearly emigration will be reduced to 10,000 at most. For the decade, this involves an estimated increase in employment of 78,000.

3. Emphasize education, training, and other forms of "human investment."

4. Recognize Ireland's obligation to aid less developed countries.

5. Continue to respect the basic principles underlying the First Program.

Agriculture

Target figures are:

1. An annual rate of increase of 3.8 per cent in agricultural production so that in 1970 gross agricultural product will be about 30 per cent greater than in 1964.

2. An annual average rise in output per person of 5.3 per cent in agriculture so that by 1970 agriculture will contribute 21 per cent to GDP.

The Second Program gives more emphasis to agricultural demand factors than the First, and notes that:

> The fundamental problem confronting Irish agriculture at the present time is that, while the capacity exists to expand production substantially, current international trading conditions favor the profitable disposal of only certain forms of additional output. [23]

The target figures are based on the hopeful assumption that during the second half of the 1960's:

> ...international market arrangements for our agricultural products (which at present, due to reasons outside the control of the government are unsatisfactory) will be considerably improved, as a result, *inter alia,* of our being admitted to membership of the European Economic Community. [24]

Means of aiding goal achievement within the power of the government include:

1. Increased emphasis upon trade agreements, particularly with Britain.

2. Increased production through further expansion and wider utilization of the agricultural and advisory services, which will be involved in state-sponsored research programs and agricultural education.

3. Continued improvement of marketing arrangements with the eventual goal of adjusting to Common Market requirements.

4. Raising of the cattle output from 1,046,000 in 1960 (1,065,000 in 1962) to 1,500,000 in 1970—an increase of 43 per cent—through the elimination of bovine tuberculosis and continued improvement in fertilizing, managing and stocking of grasslands, farm buildings, and disease control. This involves continuation of the scheme begun in the First Program of subsidies on fertilizers and grants for farm buildings and land improvement.

5. Encouragement of increased efficiency in the dairying industry, especially at the farm and creamery levels, including rationalization, and diversification of products where necessary.

6. Raising the quality of pigs through expansion of the Pig Progeny Testing arrangements and the Accredited Herds Scheme.

7. Encouragement of efficient management in pig raising and processing and continuation of subsidies on feed grains.

8. Encouragement of lamb and wool production, processing, and marketing, and expansion of programs aimed at raising the output of early lamb, and improving wool yield and quality.

9. Full government support for expansion in horticulture, including grants, government research, and education.

10. Introduction of schemes to assure that idle or underworked land is made available to strengthen the position of those underemployed on inadequate acreage, with the over-all goal of a farm unit of 40-45 acres of good land.

11. Promotion of more intensive use of land to raise income levels on the smaller family farms.

12. Expansion of agricultural credit schemes, including a hire-purchase arrangement at favorable rates for agricultural plants and machinery.

Forestry

1. Continuation of the planting program of 25,000 acres annually, subject to available land.

2. Additional measures to be added to those begun in 1958 to increase efficiency and promote timber production.

3. Attention by the Industrial Development Authority to assuring outlets for timber products.

Fisheries

1. Provision for suitable vessels, for trained skippers and crews, for adequate harbors, and for effective sales promotion in home and export markets as provided for in the Program of Sea Fisheries Development announced in a White Paper in April, 1962. This program includes:

   a) Substantial grants through An Bord Iascaigh Mhara for purchase of boats and engines.

b) Urgent attention to training of men.

c) Regional advisory service to improve fishing techniques and promote cooperation among fishermen.

d) Expenditure on research, including establishment of a Fisheries Research Station.

e) Annual grant-in-aid of £ 75,000 to Ireland Fisheries Trust for several years for development of game fishing, coarse fishing and sea angling.

Industry

The success of the Second Program hinges mainly upon the industrial sector's ability to underwrite future expansion in GNP and provide increased employment. Should the agricultural sector falter, based as it is on a tenuous assumption in regard to improved conditions in world agricultural trade, the burden upon the industrial sector will be even greater. Moreover, the success of the industrial program is seen as depending upon exports, a variable which is at least partly outside the control of the government. Over-all goals in this sector are: industrial development and adaptation to a world moving toward freer trade. These goals include:

1. Attention to the "deepening and broadening" of the industrial base.

2. Emphasis upon export development as the "key to national prosperity."

3. Emphasis upon increased efficiency needed to compete under competitive conditions resulting from lower tariffs.

The over-all target figures are:

1. An increase in industrial output of 7.1 per cent annually from 1964 to 1970. This growth will come from an estimated average annual increase in productivity of just over 4 per cent and in employment of 3 per cent. The 7.1 per cent annual growth rate corresponds to the rate actually achieved over the First Program period.

2. The target figure for industrial exports is forecast to rise 150 per cent from £ 51.1 million in 1960 to £ 125.2 million in 1970. This is a larger growth than achieved under the First Program in absolute terms. The growth is seen as crucial to the success of the Second Program inasmuch as exports must compensate for increased imports expected under freer trade, and retain their role as a growth sector and provider of employment achieved under the First Program.

The breakdown of growth targets for industrial groups appears in the following table.

TABLE 4

GROWTH TARGETS FOR INDUSTRIAL GROUPS

Industry Group	Net Output			
	(1) Value in 1960 £'000	(2) Annual average % change in volume −1958/63	(3) Projected annual average % change in volume −1960/70	(4) Required annual average % change in volume −1964/70
1 Food	28,623	5.2	4.1	3.5
2 Drink and tobacco	16,774	1.9	2.2	2.4
3 Textiles	13,132	11.0	5.4	4.0
4 Clothing and footwear	10,663	6.3	5.3	5.1
5 Wood, furniture, brushes and brooms	3,913	4.6	5.7	6.4
6 Paper and printing	12,288	6.1	5.4	4.8
7 Chemicals and chemical products	5,771	11.0	11.0	11.9
8 Structural clay products, glass, cement, etc.	5,535	11.6	10.5	10.2
9 Metal and engineering (including transport equipment)	18,851	12.7	11.2	11.0
10 Other manufacturing industries	8,521	13.6	15.1	18.3
11 Mining and quarrying (including turf)	6,491	11.5	9.0	9.6
12 Building and construction, and service-type industries	{ 24,100 { 19,014	} 5.9* }	4.9 } 6.6 }	5.6**
1-10 inclusive. Total manufacturing	124,070	7.5	7.3	7.5
1-11 inclusive. Total transportable goods	130,561	7.6	7.4	7.6
1-12 inclusive. Total all industries	173,675	7.2	7.0	7.1

* 1958/61.   ** 1962/70.

NOTES: (1) The figures in columns (2) and (4) are provisional as the output figures
           for 1963 on which they are based are themselves provisional.

       (2) The figures in columns (2) and (4) for group 10 − "Other manufacturing
           industries" − allow for the contribution to industrial growth from new
           firms whose establishment will be encouraged by industrial grants
           during the second program but whose applications for grants have not
           yet been approved.

       (3) These figures relate only to firms covered by the Census of Industrial
           Production. The figure for the net output of the industrial sector in
           1970 is based on these, after adjustment (a) to take account of small
           firms excluded from the CIP, (b) to allow for depreciation and (c) to
           eliminate double counting.

Source: *Second Program for Economic Expansion,* Part II, Dublin: Stationery Office,
        1964, p. 144.

Growth targets for industrial groups are based upon the following factors:

1. The growth in home consumption of the industry's products based upon income elasticities of demand estimates.

2. Problems and conditions in the industries examined in the industry reports prepared by the Committee on Industrial Organization.

3. Past experience in the various industries since 1953.

4. The prospect of new firms being attracted into particular industrial sectors by the various inducements offered by the government.

5. Projections for growth of food consumption and demand made by the Department of Agriculture.

Specific measures for carrying out goals for industrial groups include government action as follows:

1. Assessment by government of the comparative efficiency of Irish industry and the areas of needed improvement through such organizations as the Committee on Industrial Organization, and recommendations for correcting these comparative weaknesses.

2. Generous grants and special loan facilities toward the cost of re-equipment and adaptation. Under the Technical Assistance Scheme, grants are available of up to 50 per cent of the cost of engaging industrial consultants and of sending management and labor on training courses. Where firms are adapting to meet free trading conditions *An Foras Tionscal* (The Grant Board) assists with grants covering up to 25 per cent of the cost, or, a firm not receiving a grant may apply to the Industrial Credit Company for a special loan with waiver of interest payments and deferment of capital repayments for up to five years.

3. Encouragement of research and development by encouraging the relatively small Irish firms to cooperate in research and development programs, and assisting and supplementing the efforts of Irish firms through the auspices of the Institute for Industrial Research and Standards.

4. The cutting of tariffs by progressive reductions so that a reduction of the order of one-third is achieved by January, 1965. The purpose of such cuts is twofold: (a) to afford a stimulus to efficiency, and (b) to assure improved outlets for exports. The Second Program indicates more selective action than that of tariff-cutting will be taken in industries not taking steps toward improvement. These measures were not spelled out, however. The costs of change resulting from the lowering of tariffs will be shared by the community in three ways.

    a) Grants, special loans, and accelerated depreciation are given to encourage firms to switch to new lines of production.

    b) Where areas are adversely affected because of dependence upon firms unable to survive the new economic environment, new industries will be attracted to the area by industrial grants.

    c) Workers who lose their employment will be retrained for employment in industries which are expanding and will be assisted in moving to areas where they can obtain employment.

5. Non-repayable industrial grants up to two-thirds of the cost of fixed assets to attract "major industries" now lacking, and needed to "broaden and deepen" the industrial base, with special emphasis on the growth of major industrial centers and the establishment of industrial estates at these centers.

6. Introduction of amending legislation to extend the ten years' 100 per cent tax relief on exports "beyond 1974/75."

7. Repeal of the Control of Manufactures legislation (aimed mainly at foreign investment).

8. The planning of increased activity, and hence availability of resources, for the Industrial Development Authority so that efforts to attract new industry to Ireland, which were vastly intensified under the First Program, may continue to increase.

9. An enlarged manpower policy designed to explore labor supply, mobility, and training and retraining needs arising from the conditions of growth and change anticipated under the Second Program.

10. The planning for physical facilities and space use designed to assure an adequate capital infrastructure for industrial expansion and identify development centers of economic and social growth.

11. Continuation of the gearing of government capital programs to the needs of industrial expansion; average annual capital expenditures are forecast to rise by 60 per cent over the average annual expenditures of the First Program.

12. Raising of the supply of primary energy by at least one-third by 1970. This includes:

    a) An increase of 105 per cent over 1960's electricity generating capacity by 1970.

    b) By 1970, an increase of 200 per cent over 1960's turf (peat) production. This means *Bord na Mona's* three briquette factories will be operating at an output raised to an annual rate of 300,000 tons during the first few years of the Program and exports will reach 50,000 tons a year. Expansion will be accompanied by increased mechanization and improved methods of production.

c) Consideration before 1970 of the economies of extending oil re- finery capacity, which is insufficient at present to service demand in 1970 when oil, it is estimated, will be a source of almost one- half the country's total primary energy requirements.

d) Encouragement of efficiency of fuel use as a result of the growing dependence on imported fuels, and continued surveillance of the economies of nuclear energy. Fuel efficiency survey grants will be increased from one-third to one-half.

13. Assessment of the needs of transport from the standpoint of the target for a 50 per cent increase in GNP by 1970 over 1960's GNP, and the need for economic allocation of investment among airlines, railways, roads, and shipping.

14. A doubling of tourist income between 1960 and 1970, assisted in various ways such as traffic promotion by *Bord Failte;* loans, tax allowances, and grants towards expansion and improvements of hotels and resorts; completion of the ten-year scheme begun under the First Program for the development of major resorts, and grants for provision of entertainment facilities at these resorts; and better ferry service between England and Ireland.

15. Provision of sufficient capital for efficient development of telephone service as the economy expands.

Services

In the services area the government's policies on education, transport, and tourism are expected to contribute to growth goals. In addition, the government will attempt to increase the efficiency of wholesale and retail trade distribution through advisory-consultative groups. For the most part, however, it is implied that the expected 43 per cent increase in services from 1960 to 1970 will be an automatic result of other expansion areas, particularly the expansion of the industrial sector. Should the service sector develop as expected under the Second Program, it will entail an annual rate of increase of 3.6 per cent for the sector, and provide an estimated increase in employ- ment in this sector of 14 per cent, so that the number engaged in this sector will be 58,000 greater than in 1960, a figure that represents almost 70 per cent of the total net increase in employment envisioned by the plan.

SUMMARY

In summary, Ireland's experience with a lightly structured planning technique designed to induce action through government leadership rather than impose action by government edict has been remarkably successful to date in disturbing the forces of inertia which have inactivated the Irish economy for ages, and has created conditions conducive to industrial growth over the past six years. The Irish have been in the enviable position where rather obvious actions that would be conducive to industrial expansion are discernible, and the agglomerate of action necessary to get something started is not so large as to be beyond the means of a well-coordinated government program of considered alternatives that eliminates projects of minimal priority. Ireland's stable political situation contributed to the successful application of techniques of planning patterned after the French variety, and enabled it to choose this type of planning in the first place.

The over-all goals of the First Program—to stem the flow of emigration and expand industrially in preparation for European Economic Community membership—were successfully met to the extent that the first five years were expected to be only foundation-laying years. The success of the First Program was, in fact, beyond that anticipated, to a great degree as a result of the large influx of foreign investment that raised industrial exports by over 90 per cent. Whereas the First Program foresaw the needed increase in saving to finance industrial investment as being financed mainly by domestic saving, it has been financed to a large degree by foreign capital. Current saving rose from £ 59.5 million in 1960 to £ 81 million in 1963, or £ 21.3 million. Dominant in this increase was the increase in company savings as opposed to personal savings. The foreign capital inflow increased from £ .8 million in 1960 to £ 22 million in 1963, or £ 22.2 million. The 6.5 per cent increase in total investment envisioned as necessary to achieve the 50 per cent GNP increase by 1970 aimed at under the Second Program has been exceeded, and investment as a percentage of GNP moved from 14.6 per cent of GNP in 1960 to 18.4 per cent in 1964.

Under the Second Program, industry is again expected to be the main agent of economic expansion. Moreover, the Second Program states, "Because of a small home market, it is mainly through exports that economic expansion can be achieved."[25] The Second Program's success hinges upon the targets for industrial growth, since agriculture can provide neither the increased employment needed, nor the increased value of exports, and the service sector's success is dependent upon the success of the industrial sector. The need for the continuation in growth of industrial exports has led to the extension under the Second Program of the measures taken under the First Program to attract foreign capital and spur exports. The next chapter turns more specifically to the implementation techniques emphasized under the planning setup in Ireland which are designed to achieve the all-important goal of industrial expansion.

Notes

1. Pierre Masse, "Why France Adopted National Planning After the War, and the Advantages She Sees in Retaining it," *French and Other National Economic Plans for Growth,* Paris: The European Committee for Economic and Social Progress (CEPES), June, 1963, p. 6.

2. See M. Valery Giscard D'Estaing, Minister of Finance and Economic Affairs, "Presentation of the Fourth Plan" in *The Fourth Modernization and Equipment Plan, Statements Before the National Assembly,* French Affairs - No. 139, June, 1962, p. 8.

3. *Ibid.,* p. 15.

4. Stanislaw Wellisz, "Economic Planning in the Netherlands, France, and Italy," *Journal of Political Economy,* LXVIII (June, 1960), 252.

5. *Ibid.,* p. 268

6. John Sheahan, *Promotion and Control of Industry in Postwar France,* Cambridge, Massachusetts: Harvard University Press, 1963, p. 198.

7. Gunnar Myrdal, *Economic Theory and Underdeveloped Regions,* London: Gerald Duckworth and Company, Limited, 1957, p. 84.

8. The terms "plan" and "program" are used interchangeably in this study. What in other countries might be labeled a five-year plan, is called by the Irish a five-year program.

9. *Op. cit.; French and Other National Economic Plans for Growth,* p. 37.

10. *Economic Development,* Dublin: Stationery Office, 1958, 253 pp.

11. John P. Lewis, *Notes on the Nurture of Country Planning,* Bulletin published by the Bureau of Business Research, Graduate School of Business, Indiana University, 1962, p. 13.

12. *Second Program for Economic Expansion,* Part I, Dublin: Stationery Office, 1963, p. 7.

13. *Program for Economic Expansion,* Dublin: Stationery Office, November, 1958, p. 8.

14. *Ibid.,* p. 34.

15. *Ibid.,* p. 40

16. The services sector covers that part of GNP arising outside agriculture, forestry, fishing, and industry, but excluding certain service-type industries covered by the Census of Industrial Production, e.g., public utilities such as electricity and gas.

17. The source for the above figures is *Second Program for Economic Expansion,* Part II, Dublin: Stationery Office, 1964, 340 pp.

18. Sources for the above figures are *Economic Statistics Issued Prior to the Budget 1963,* Dublin: Stationery Office, 1963, pp. 26-28; and *Ireland,* Paris: OECD Economic Survey, 1964, p. 24.

19. *Op. cit., Second Program for Economic Expansion,* Part I, p. 8.

20. *Ibid.,* p. 11.

21. *Ibid.,* p. 8.

22. *Op. cit., Ireland,* p. 5.

23. *Op. cit., Second Program for Economic Expansion,* Part I, p. 24.

24. *Ibid.,* p. 22.

25. *Ibid.,* p. 10.

CHAPTER **4** GOVERNMENTAL
MACHINERY FOR
INFLUENCING INVESTMENT

The lightness of governmental planning machinery is one of the defining characteristics of the type of planning adopted in Ireland. Congeniality of planning with a market economy and Irish democratic institutions rests in part upon the confined role played by government controls, agencies, and departments. A limit to the hierarchical network of the governmental planning apparatus also works hand-in-glove with the philosophy of participant planning. This philosophy rests on the assumption that support is gained and efforts extended on behalf of the plan in direct relation to the participation by the various groups of the society in the design of the plan.

Reliance upon indirect implementation tools such as tariff-cutting, grants, and tax remission that work through the price system has minimized the need for large expansions of governmental machinery for planning purposes. No legislation was enacted to create and staff a paramount agency of government devoted solely to planning, with authority to hand down prescriptions to other units of government and the private sector. The very informality of the process of planning is striking. The planners have carried out their policies of influencing new investment by working in cooperation with existing institutions.

The planning activities of the government in Ireland are centered around the Department of Finance. Heading the planning efforts is a professor of economics on leave from Trinity College, Dublin. He works with a very small staff of civil servants drawn from the Department of Finance. The Department of Industry and Commerce has also become heavily involved in the planning process. Economists in government, industry, and private foundations have advised and worked with the planners. Planning proceeds in consultation with the *Taoiseach* (Prime Minister), the ultimate coordinator, who places the completed document before the parliament as a major policy instrument.

In general, there is support for planning by the political parties in Ireland, and there have been no votes of confidence called over the series of legislative measures emanating from the first two plans.

The attention given to planning goals and needs by the *Taoiseach* in the budget facilitates and reinforces the efforts of the planners to implement the plan. Some government bodies have been more heavily endowed as a result of planning activities, and enlarged, but they are not subject to central planning authority. The planners must seek support for the plan and coordination among government agencies and departments in line with plan needs through persuasion rather than authority. The same statement applies to control by the planners of the investment of state trading bodies, i.e., government enterprises.

Certain of the government entities whose resources have been enlarged with the advent of planning are concerned with the influencing of private industrial investment. These include the Industrial Development Authority, The Export Board, the Shannon Free Airport Development Company, Limited, The Industrial Credit Company, Limited, and the Grant Board. Consultation between industry and the government planners is another avenue for influencing private investment.

CONSULTATION WITH INDUSTRY

Government-industry consultations have followed, not preceded, publication of plan targets. In fact, meaningful participation by the private sector in reviewing industry targets first began under the Second Program. The government forecast growth rates based upon industry data from the Central Statistics Office and other government sources, and incorporated these forecasts into Part I of the Second Program published in August, 1963. A review and revision of these targets with industry were instituted in early 1964.

Delay of the consultation aspect of planning was born of necessity rather than design. The five years of the First Program were formative years in the development of planning machinery. The government did not have the personnel, experience, information, or channels of contact prerequisite to the execution of a more encompassing plan such as the Second Program. The First Program concentrated on the public sector where coordination of action with plan goals was more readily established.

The necessary groundwork was laid during the First Program for participation by industry in target goals. Committees were set up, drawing qualified personnel from industry, government, and the universities, to make detailed surveys of all of the major industrial sectors of Ireland. The Department of Industry and Commerce, working with the Federation of Irish Industries, started the laborious task of persuading traditionally suspicious Irish firms to come together and form industrial adaptation councils to discuss the actions needed to smooth the transition period following the lowering of tariffs.

By November of 1964 consultation and review of the program projections of 1970 output, employment, exports, and imports had proceeded to the point where a report was issued on the results. The report states the over-all differences between the program's targets for industrial output and employment and the projections obtained from consultation with industry were very small, and discussions were considered by the government as a confirmation of its Second Program employment and output targets. Export and import forecasts before and after consultations were divergent, however. Estimates based on the results of discussions with industry were 20 per cent higher for both imports and exports. Comments upon the new export and import estimates reflecting the thinking of the government appear in the report. The planners feel industrialists tend to see lower tariffs as bringing in more competitive imports than is realistic, and overestimate export figures as a result of thinking of exports in terms of growth rates needed to replace losses in home sales under free trade.[1]

As indicated, the Irish planners fully appreciate the importance of a continuing dialogue between government and industry to the setting of plan targets, the meeting of plan targets, and the review and revision of plan targets:

> ...economic programming, by its very nature, is a flexible and continuous process....The targets, and the policies which support them, must be regarded as an adjustable scaffolding which will support and guide the economy....the flexible, timely and rational adaptation and modification of the framework of the second program is an essential element in its effective execution. The problem, therefore, is to ensure that adequate information is available to indicate what modifications and changes should be made, especially in the targets and policies for the industrial sector.[2]

Tardiness in setting up consultations resulted from the slow evolution of industrial organizations for conferring, and a shortage of personnel. Once begun, the consultations often proved to be a vehicle through which the government could influence industry thinking. Hoped-for outgrowths of the consultations are improved managerial performance, an increase in industry statistics and in long-range management planning based on these statistics, and a continuous orientation of management thinking along lines that will contribute most to economic expansion. Plans have been made for annual reviews of industrial performance concentrating upon the difficulties each industry experiences as it seeks to achieve plan targets. This will provide a feedback to the government of industry problems and potentials as times passes and changes occur. Additional efforts to improve organizational and procedural approaches to consultation are under way in order to develop a smooth back-and-forth flow of information that is currently lacking. There is a need to give labor a more defined role in these discussions. To date, labor's participation has been very limited.

PUBLIC ENTERPRISE

The investment of public enterprises was a prime area of concentration in the First Program. This sector of the economy invited the planners' attention for two reasons. First, past investment in social areas such as housing was large enough to afford a change of emphasis to public investment in production facilities without undesirable political repercussions for the party in power. Secondly, the public enterprise sector of Ireland was developed to the extent that it could serve as a ready-made network for increasing industrial investment. The planners turned to this instrument at hand to begin efforts aimed at industrializing the economy.

Public enterprises extant at the beginning of planning in 1958 which could be considered directly involved in industrial output, or the creation of infrastructure directly related to the industrialization of the economy, were as follows:

Name	Principle activity
1. *Arramara Teo*	Carrageen and sea-rod meal production
2. Board for the Employment of the Blind	Manufacture of baskets, cane furniture, mats, and mattresses
3. *Bord Iascaigh Mhara* (Sea Fisheries Board)	Development of sea-fishing industry, including fishing, fish processing, etc.
4. *Bord na Mona* (Peat Production Board)	Turf, turf briquettes, peat moss production
5. *Ceimici Teo* (Industrial Alcohol Board)	Industrial alcohol, glucose, potato starch, and potato pulp
6. *Comhlucht Siuicre Eireann Teo* (Irish Sugar Co.)	Production of sugar, ground limestone golden syrup, processed fruits and vegetables
7. Dairy Disposal Co., Ltd. and subsidiaries	Butter, milk powder, cheese, condensed milk, and toffee production
8. Electricity Supply Board	Electricity production
9. *Gaeltarra Eireann*	Production of tweed, toys, etc.
10. Irish Steel Holdings, Ltd.	Steel and galvanized sheet
11. *Aer Rianta Teo, Aer Lingus Teo, and Aerlinte Eireann Teo*	Air services

Name	Principle activity
12. *Coras Iompair Eireann*	Rail, road, and water transport, and harbor management
13. Irish Shipping Limited	Ocean freight services

New productive enterprises established after 1958 were *Min-Fheir Teo* (Grass Meal Ltd.) which produces grass meal on drained bogland, and *Nitrigin Eireann Teo,* which produces nitrogenous fertilizers.

The cooperative spirit has been dutifully courted in the state's expansion programs by explicitly stating the state's position *vis-a-vis* public investment, and by carrying out programs with due respect to continuity in the state's role. Thus, the First Program states: "The government favors the system of private ownership of industry and will not be disposed to enter any manufacturing field in which private enterprise is already operating successfully."[3] This program, as outlined in Chapter 3, was essentially a redirection of public investment toward productive capital expenditure and not a vast increase in the role of the state. While twelve new state-sponsored bodies originated during the 1958-61 period, none, with the exception of the industry for the production of nitrogenous fertilizer, were large investment projects of an industrial nature. Rather, the state moved to originate state entities in the fields of marketing, research, and promotion and development designed to encourage and attract private enterprise, or enlarge the role of existing bodies in this area. For example, *Coras Trachtala Teo,* a state body which facilitates the marketing of Irish goods in foreign markets, was given permanent status in 1959 and its resources expanded so that it could make additional efforts to increase exports in line with plan goals.

In summary, the state's role as producer, promoter, financier, and marketeer has been left open, within the limits of continuity with past actions by the government, to move into areas necessary for reasonable economic expansion as outlined in the programs, when these activities are not undertaken by private enterprise because of large risks involved, private lethargy, or other deterrents. In seeking its goals of increased industrial investment the government has been able to draw upon its cadre of already established bodies in such areas as steel, communications and transportation, tourist activities, sugar and food processing, turf production, and electricity to "extend their activities into projects related to their main spheres of operation and to test the profitability of new lines and new markets," justified by the reasoning that "no fund of experience, enterprise, or management ability can be allowed to lie dormant, if the maximum rate of development is to be attained."[4] It may be added that in the past in Ireland, as in other countries, the government has entered various industrial fields as a result of private failures, and under pressure to continue employment opportunities where private operations have decided to withdraw their capital investment.

In 1958/59 public capital expenditure other than social capital amounted
to £ 27.67 million.[5] The period of the First Program saw public capital
expenditure of a non-social nature jump to £ 56.56 by 1963/64. Social capital
also doubled in this period, moving from £ 10.22 to £ 21.94. Thus, the relative
shares held steady over the program, while non-social capital increases expanded the greatest in absolute amounts. These public capital figures include
land acquisition and credit.

The Second Program estimates a total public capital expenditure figure
for 1964/65 of £ 96.11, a gradual decline to £ 92.82 million in 1968/69 because of timing of needed expenditures, and an increase in 1969/70 to only
slightly above the 1964/65 level, that is to £ 97.32 million. Non-social public
capital expenditure is forecast at declining absolute and relative rates, drop-
ping from £ 66.89 in 1964/65 to £ 60.10 million in 1969/70.

Two factors should be noted here: (a) expenditures during the First Program were 35 per cent higher than anticipated, and (b) the increased expenditure on social capital forecast in the Second Program has distinct political
overtones. Nevertheless, if the anticipated trend is realized, the per cent
of total gross fixed capital formation in the industrial sector that is controlled
by the government could be expected to decline in subsequent years up to
1970 from the estimated 1958/59 figure of 38 per cent. The public sector, if
it moves along with plan forecasts, will have shown no drastic break with the
past, but will have maintained continuity, increasing public investment for
industrial endeavors long enough to spur industrialization and a rise in GNP,
and then reverting to social investment emphasis. Moreover, the total amount
of public investment is seen as leveling off over the Second Program rather
than increasing apace of GNP increases.

TAX REMISSION ON EXPORTS

Goods manufactured in Ireland and exported are allowed export profits
tax relief by authorization under the Finance Act of 1956, as subsequently
amended through 1961. This provision applies to all new companies, and to
profits derived from increased export trade over the exports of the standard
period, which is either of the two years 1955 or 1956. While export profits
tax relief was 50 per cent in 1956, it has subsequently been raised, so that
full exemption from tax on profits attributable to export trade in Irish-manu-
factured goods is given for ten consecutive years from the first year in which
the company engages in export business or from the second "year of assessment" as the company elects. In the case of a new business the profits
assessed in the second year of assessment would be the profits of the first
full year of trading.

Currently, there is a limit to the period during which the full ten years'
relief can be claimed so that a firm must be established or eligible for begin-

ning tax relief by April of 1964 in order to obtain ten full years of 100 per cent tax relief. However, the tax relief incentive has produced results beyond original expectations, and the Second Program recommends enabling legislation to extend the period.

In addition to the ten years of full relief, there is a period of partial relief for five years. In the first year (that is, the eleventh year of tax relief) the tax payable on profits attributable to export trade will be reduced by 80 per cent, and in the second year 65 per cent, the third 50 per cent, the fourth 35 per cent and the fifth and last year of tax relief, 15 per cent.

More lenient tax relief is given to firms locating on the Shannon Industrial Estate, and this subsidy is discussed below under the Shannon Free Airport Development Company, Limited.

SHANNON FREE AIRPORT DEVELOPMENT COMPANY, LIMITED

The Shannon Development Company was set up by the government in 1959 as a means of preserving the Shannon Airport, threatened with extinction by the introduction of jet aircraft which no longer needed a refueling stop enroute to Europe. The major activities of the company have been in three areas—industrial development through the mechanism of an industrial estate at the airport which affords custom-free entry and exit of goods, travel promotion, and warehousing activities. Shannon Airport is located in the relatively underdeveloped area of Western Ireland which has experienced large outflows of population from a farming region unable to provide employment opportunities on the farm. The fact that the industrial estate was able to attract sixteen foreign firms to the estate between 1959 and the summer of 1964 attests to the fact that it has also contributed to the over-all planning goals of increasing exports and providing employment opportunities in Ireland for the workers leaving the farms.

The assets of the company are mainly in the form of factory buildings built for leasing to prospective tenants, dwellings erected for persons employed at the estate, and land held for future expansion. Financial incentives given to firms locating at Shannon Estate include non-repayable cash grants and tax-free profits. Cash grants during the first three years of operation totaled approximately £ 500,000. These incentives are given on the following terms:

1. Machinery Grants: Cash grants covering up to 50 per cent of the cost of factory machinery and equipment are made available to suitable firms.

2. Grants for Worker Training: Cash grants are given toward the cost of training Irish workers to perform tasks of employment with firms located on the estate.

3. Tax Exemption: Under government legislation tax exemption is granted for all profits arising from export business until 1983.

Profits accrued may be freely repatriated to the investing country, as is
the case in general with tax exemption in Ireland. And, of course, as the name
indicates, all goods imported and intended for re-export enter and leave
customs-free and without customs supervision except a simplified report on
inventory accounting.

The selection of the size of subsidies allowed to individual firms and
the type of subsidies (grants as well as tax remission) appears to be based
upon the strategy that they should be generous enough to counteract competing subsidies from other countries, and assure the measure of success needed
immediately to keep the airport in operation. As far as discernible, there
seems to have been no detailed study of the best type of subsidy (or subsidies) for attracting firms with the least public outlay. Moreover, the company has not yet developed specific criteria for choosing recipients of the
subsidies. Chapter 6 deals with evidence pointing to the fact that subsidies
may be higher than needed at Shannon Estate to do the job Shannon Development Company has been assigned.[6]

GRANTS AND THEIR ADMINISTRATION

Grants are administered by *An Foras Tionscal,* a government corporation
set up in 1952 under the Undeveloped Areas Act, and originally devoted to
administering grants on a relatively small scale to companies willing to
locate in areas of Ireland designated as "undeveloped." In 1959 new power
and funds were made available to *An Foras Tionscal* under the Industrial
Grants Act in line with the first expansion program's efforts to provide incentive for new industrial investment. This corporation now handles all
industrial grants except those administered by the Shannon Development
Company for firms locating at the Shannon Estate.

Grants of up to two-thirds of the cost of a factory site, site development,
factory building, machinery, plant and equipment are available from *An Foras
Tionscal.* Grants in excess of £ 250,000 cannot exceed one-half of the total
amount of such costs, or a sum equivalent to £ 1,000 multiplied by the number of persons that in the opinion of *An Foras Tionscal* will be employed by
the firm seeking the grant, whichever is the less. Grants in excess of £ 500,000
require the consent of the Minister for Industry and Commerce and the Minister
for Finance. In addition, *An Foras Tionscal* administers the adaptation grants
which are to expire in 1965, and are the carrot to go with the stick of tariff
reduction to enable Irish firms to become fully competitive. These moderni-

zation and expansion grants may not exceed 25 per cent of the cost of the enlargement or adaptation.

Grants are not given to foreign firms that will compete in the domestic market with Irish manufacturers. *An Foras Tionscal* will also look to see that the firm receiving grants has a "reasonable degree" of financial risk in the business. There are no strings attached to the grants, and only two general conditions that must be fulfilled: (a) the principals involved must not sell their investment for a period of five years without the consent of *An Foras Tionscal,* and (b) the principals must not sell the fixed assets for a period of ten years without the consent of *An Foras Tionscal.*

Prior to 1959, *An Foras Tionscal* had few firms to which it could give away money. Then with the advent of 100 per cent tax remission, and increased efforts of the Industrial Development Authority to attract foreign firms, grants were allocated to those new foreign firms that did not compete with home production and contributed to the plan goals of expanding exports and employment. This does not mean that domestic industry is not eligible; rather the concentration of grants to new foreign firms results from the fact that Irish enterprise has not come forward in large numbers with proposals to contribute, in a manner which *An Foras Tionscal* judges to be potentially successful, to the field of exports or, for that matter, to new home market production,

Almost all of the 133 new industrial undertakings with foreign participation begun during the First Program received industrial grants, and almost all export 100 per cent of their output, which means they are also eligible to receive subsidies in the form of 100 per cent tax relief on profits for ten years. The Second Program states that the efforts, successful under the First Program, of the Industrial Development Authority and *An Foras Tionscal* working in tandem to attract industry from abroad and encourage projects that can compete in free trade conditions will be intensified, and needed funds made available.[7]

More specific criteria for selecting grant recipients than outlined above apparently are not developed or in use. *An Foras Tionscal* is generally more closely allied with the promotion of development goals as outlined under the expansion programs than is the Industrial Credit Company, perhaps since the scope and purpose of its operations have varied in direct relationship to planning policies. Approximately £ 12 million in grants were administered during the First Program; there have been nine failures of firms receiving grants on the official records. Administration is carried out by approximately six employees, and the annual budget runs approximately £ 10,500. Since specific criteria are not laid down for the administration of grants, discretion resides with the staff of *An Foras Tionscal.* Ireland is a country noted for the honesty of its public servants!

INDUSTRIAL CREDIT

The Industrial Credit Company, Limited underwrites capital issues and serves as an issuing house for capital flotations, provides long-term and medium-term secured loans, and offers hire-purchase facilities for new industrial plant and machinery. It was incorporated in 1933 to promote the development of the capital market and complement private financial institutions by providing services that would promote industrial investment when such services were not offered by private institutions.

The conditions of borrowing may vary from case to case, but with the exception noted below, borrowing is done on a commercial, non-subsidized basis, the current interest charge on long-term capital being 7 per cent. Loans which in fact subsidize new investment are available up to March 31, 1965, as an alternative to adaptation grants from *An Foras Tionscal*. The Industrial Credit Company may finance up to 75 per cent of the cost of fixed assets on the basis that repayment will not begin for a period of up to five years at specially reduced interest rates, or under the conditions that interest payments are deferred for a period of up to three years. The Industrial Credit Company will grant this type of loan only where the investment will make the company fully competitive under free trading conditions.

The Company has not lacked for funds since the Industrial Credit Act of 1959 which authorized the company to increase its share capital by £ 5 million, and increased the Company's borrowing powers to £ 15 million. With the increased industrial investment of the First Program the Company's provision of capital picked up considerably. A total of approximately £ 17.5 million of capital was provided for industry from September 1, 1958, to October 31, 1963, in the form of underwriting, investments, loans, and hire-purchase capital.

In 1964 a new and "separate" finance company was set up under the name of *Taisci Stait Teoranta*. It will be financed directly from the Exchequer, but will be managed by the Industrial Credit Company. At least two important factors contributed to the establishment of this new arrangement: first, the planning authority in Ireland has stated in its programs that there is a need for "basic" industry to "deepen" the industrial base. Intertwined with the thinking about the need for certain large-scale industrial projects is the feeling that these undertakings often involve such a degree of risk in the Irish environment as to preclude the establishment of a private company without assumption of part of the risk by the government. Secondly, it was apparent that in such cases it would be politically unwise, given the concern over the returns received from the giving away of public funds without strings attached, to attract foreign participation and know-how simply by the device of grants. This gave rise to the arrangement of loans to supplement grants where the absolute amount of government funds involved would be large, and a scheme for possible government equity participation. The Second Program outlines the provision of loans by *Taisci Stait Teoranta* as follows:

> Special arrangements were introduced for projects involving grants of over £ 250,000. In these cases, the maximum grant is £ 1,000 per worker, or half the cost of the fixed assets, whichever is the less. However, subject to the industrialist providing not less than one-third of the cost of the fixed assets, the balance may be provided by a combination of (a) a grant within the limits mentioned; (b) a special loan; (c) a commercial loan from the Industrial Credit Co. equal to the amount of the special loan. The special loan would be provided by *Taisci Stait Teoranta,* a new and separate finance company to be managed by the Industrial Credit Company but financed directly from the Exchequer. The special loan would be repayable only at the option of the industrialist, would not involve a charge on the assets, would be free of interest for 7 years and thereafter would bear interest at a rate which would increase according as ordinary dividends exceeded 7 ½ per cent. With the agreement of the industrialist, equity participation by the state could replace loan finance.[8]

Under this new arrangement, where the government has used public funds to attract capital intensive projects of a large size, the state would get back part of the money invested, and should the undertaking prove profitable, the state would receive a return on its investment. Or, if the industrialist would find equity participation by the state preferable to loan repayment, the state would be willing to accept share capital, thus forming a mixed public-private company to protect the state's interest in the undertaking. Present negotiations under way are for an aviation manufacturing plant in conjunction with a French company. The 1964/65 budget allows £ 1.5 million to *Taisci Stait Teoranta* for the aviation project. Subsequent yearly allotments are anticipated under the Second Program as being on the order of £ 0.25 per annum, and will go for "loans to large industrial undertakings and hotels to supplement grant assistance."[9] Thus, the planning authorities do not appear to forecast a large role for this type of grant-loan-equity combination; rather it appears that it evolved as an implementation tool out of concern for the giving away of large absolute sums of money to one company under the aviation development company transaction, and provided a solution to the reservations voiced by the Industrial Credit Company in regard to having "non-commercial" loans reflected on its balance sheet.

THE INDUSTRIAL DEVELOPMENT AUTHORITY

The Industrial Development Authority is a part of the civil service under the direction of the Minister for Industry and Commerce. Its chief function has been to attract industry from abroad. The Authority's role and resources were strengthened after planning began. Attraction of foreign capital was facilitated by the repeal of legislation designed to discourage foreign investment.

The Irish often accuse their civil servants of being tradition-bound. However, the performance of this body has been exemplary in respect to aggressiveness, innovation, and dynamism. The emphasis of the plan upon foreign investment has resulted in the Authority being heavily involved in plan fulfillment. Moreover, the participation by the Department of Industry and Commerce in the planning efforts has established a direct link between the planners and the Industrial Development Authority. This promotional body has been an important performer in the area of attracting foreign firms. It has accomplished the challenging task of persuading foreign investors to take advantage of the opportunities available in Ireland, including the state assistance offered to new exporting firms, and has assured foreign capitalists that Ireland welcomes them. Civil servants of the Authority have been the contact men, the makers of first impressions, and the follow-through force. While this study does not focus on the contributions made by the Industrial Development Authority, their role is recognized as a necessary condition for the success of implementation tools of planning such as government subsidies and tax remission.

Notes

1. National Industrial Economic Council, *Report on Results of Discussions with Industry on the Second Program Targets,* Dublin: Stationery Office, November, 1964, p. 14.

2. National Industrial Economic Council, *Report on Procedures for Continuous Review of Progress under the Second Program for Economic Expansion,* Dublin: Stationery Office, June, 1964, p. 8.

3. *Program for Economic Expansion,* Dublin: Stationery Office, 1958, p.40.

4. *Ibid.,* p. 40.

5. Social investment consists of capital expenditures for housing, sanitary and miscellaneous services, schools, hospitals, and other building and construction. Investments of a non-social nature included in public capital expenditures are listed under the following categories: ports, harbors and airports, tourism, agriculture, agricultural credit, forestry, fisheries, fuel and power, telephones, transport, industry, industrial credit, and miscellaneous small expenditures of a capital nature.

6. Assuming an investment in plant and equipment of £ 300,000, no return on investment the first year of operations, and a 20 per cent return on fixed investment thereafter, and taking the average grant figure as a percentage of investment outside of Shannon of approximately 33 1/3 per cent, a

comparison of subsidies in the form of tax remission and grants for plant and equipment indicates the large differential between Shannon and the rest of the economy:

	Shannon	Rest of Ireland
Plant and Equipment	£ 300,000	£ 300,000
Grant	150,000	100,000
Tax Remission	672,480	300,829
TOTAL SUBSIDIES	£ 822,480	£ 400,829

7. *Second Program for Economic Expansion,* Part II, Dublin: Stationery Office, pp. 154-155.

8. *Ibid., p. 153.*

9. *Ibid., p. 284.*

CHAPTER **5** IMPLEMENTATION OF
PROGRAM GOALS FOR
INDUSTRIALIZATION

The concept of coordination through cooperation underlies the technique
of planning used by the Irish. Yet, the skeptic, cognizant of the hazardous
route to industrial growth any relatively unindustrialized economy must travel,
has grounds for inquiring how goals are really achieved, and what forces and
controls are working for the assurance of plan achievement. In particular,
how are industrialization goals being carried out in a country that heretofore
has depended upon agriculture as the mainstay of its economy? In what manner are the Irish implementing the key goals of industrialization that the
plans foretell as providing new jobs and higher living standards for the
people of Ireland?

CHOICE OF IMPLEMENTATION TOOLS

In essence, part of the answer to implementation lies within the spirit
of the plan and the voluntary action forthcoming from all groups in a nation
alarmed by its inevitably diminishing significance unless jobs are created in
Ireland for the people of Ireland. Consensus concerning the over-all goals,
their importance, and participation in the actual selection of targets can and
has led to a responsiveness in Ireland that has diminished the areas of needed government influence.

Voluntary private action alone, however, composes only part of the
answer to implementation. There is no assurance private goals and public
goals will be the same. If they are the same, the private sphere may not
understand this to be so. Or, if the private sector foresees its welfare as
coincident with plan goals, it may not have the financial or other abilities
requisite to carrying out plan targets in the private sphere.

If programming is not simply an invitation to action, there must be positive government measures taken to implement program goals. In fact, the
implementation aspects of planning influence the initial stages of goal setting, since they bear upon the feasibility of plan objectives. Under the French

type of planning the government must select its implementation tools carefully in order not to diminish, or lose altogether, the forces of the private
economy that can work toward plan fulfillment. The need to avoid the types
of influence and control over the economy that are generally considered un-
acceptable in Ireland led the government into areas of indirect influence—
such as the areas of finance and tariff cutting—that have effect upon the
pivotal variable of industrial investment, and yet can be made palatable to
to the groups affected.

The public sector is also an acceptable implementation tool for increasing investment in the Irish economy, so long as it does not seriously reduce
the cooperative spirit sought from the private sector. Tolerance levels of
acceptable expansion of government activity in the economy have been defined in reflection of the political-economic sentiment concerning the role of
public enterprise in Ireland. These levels of acceptance have been broad
enough to allot public enterprise an important role in Irish planning. This has
been fortunate in that all forces are needed in the predominantly agricultural
economy of Ireland to aid in the industrialization efforts.

While the general feeling in Ireland that planning should leave a large
measure of action to the private sector places limitations upon the variety of
government controls, it also lightens the performance requirements of the
government necessary for retention of political support at the polls. The
government is in part absolved from responsibility for full goal achievement
when this responsibility is divided in reflection of the general concensus of
the populace, and a portion of it is placed upon the doorstep of the private
sector. But, inasmuch as a high degree of success will visit acclaim upon the
government in power, and failure will not absolve it completely of blame, a
responsive parliamentary government such as exists in Ireland will seek
effective implementation tools for plan goal fulfillment.

It is pertinent, then, to comment upon several characteristics of importance to the effectiveness of implementation tools used in the Irish situation.
As previously emphasized, Ireland possesses a highly developed democracy,
and fortunately, in regard to the potential success of participant planning,
the country does not have the type of power structure found in some Latin
American and other underdeveloped regions, where goals of democratic political development and economic progress require efforts of almost revolutionary
proportions to undermine vested positions of power that are inimical to national development and growth. On the contrary, the existence of a socially
balanced democratic state and the respect for adherence to democratic procedures in Ireland create a commitment for the planners to respect and consider the interests of represented groups and individuals. Under the political
and economic restraints of participant planning and the highly developed
democracy of Ireland, the government will face pressures to choose implementation tools that are characterized by what might be called the four "C's"
—compatibility, continuity, cooperation, and conservation.

Techniques of achieving economic expansion under "democratic" planning must be *compatible* with existing power structures and existing institutions in the society, for example, existing pressure groups such as business and labor groups, and institutions such as private property rights. Implementation methods that would result in rather widespread disruption of patterns and hierarchies of extant institutions would violate the spirit of the cooperative approach to planning, would dissipate energies needed for propelling the economy forward, and could have long-range braking effects. The case of Soviet agriculture in part illustrates this point.

Once the nation has been aroused concerning the need for development, unnecessary tensions can be avoided in the execution of growth plans. It is inevitable, of course, that certain vested interests experience erosion of their positions with the advent of changes inherent in the industrialization process. However, on balance growth will be hopefully more of an evolutionary than a revolutionary social process. If this is to be so, the government must be concerned with *continuity*, in that the techniques for achieving plan targets must avoid violent disturbances of the socio-political-economic milieu. Such techniques will flow from the current ideological, and procedural ways of thinking and acting, and, wherever possible, work through established institutions. This means that the mix of implementation tools will be determined in part by the pre-planning situation in order to reduce friction, and, where the nation is not highly industrialized, avoid aggravating the inevitably unsettling socio-economic changes that come with transition from an agricultural to an industrial society.

In order to align all possible forces behind its expansion efforts, the government will consciously strive to create an atmosphere of participation by all groups and fair consideration of all groups. That is, the government will court *cooperation* rather than opposition in the planning process, such cooperation itself assuring target implementation to some degree. Finally, the government will seek implementation tools that afford as high a degree of leverage as possible within the framework of "democratic" planning and the limitations it poses for the extension of control techniques.

In looking over the kit of tools the Irish have used to implement their plan goals of industrialization, success of the First Program as outlined in Chapter 3 does not rest separately with any specific policy designed to further the expansion program; rather the conglomerate of actions and reactions by the government have generally been characterized by the four "C's," have been interconnected and reinforcing in their effect, and have, as a group, set the stage for the industrial "take-off."

There were, in the conditions of the Irish economy of 1957, many obvious changes that could be made, and were made, that involved relatively small government expense; there were other programs involving rather large government outlays; and there were policies for the reorientation of government expenditure. And outside of the economy, there was the existence of the

European Economic Community and England's proposed entry in the late 1950's, which provided the government with a mandate for change. Moreover, the lack of economic progress in the pre-program days does not preclude there being important prerequisites for growth in existence before 1958, one of the more notable being a stable government. It is fruitless to seek the primal cause for economic growth in one program or policy; it is quite fruitful, however, to examine rather closely particular policies that, on the basis of factual evidence that can be supported by theoretical considerations, have produced rather obvious immediate causal forces contributing to success of economic expansion goals.

Ireland is attempting to increase dramatically her industrial production. This means, of course, that policies for goal implementation have been aimed at influencing directly and indirectly the volume and composition of new investment. The success of the program has been particularly dependent upon Ireland's ability to channel investment into the export field. The more strategic policies designed to deal with the channeling of investment into industrial production, and particularly into export production, have been financial incentives such as subsidies upon exports and financial control over the granting of credit and subsidies, as well as over investment by government enterprises (see Chapter 6). These tools have played a dominant immediate causal role in the success of the Irish expansion programs.

The above is not a surprising conclusion. Indirect controls and influence over investment through monetary policies and credit policies, as well as government ownership in specified fields, have become quite acceptable areas for government action within the framework of market economies. Moreover, pressure upon investment has come to be considered an acceptable and important implementation mechanism under "democratic" planning. This is particularly true of the French type of planning after which the Irish development has been patterned. In fact, in France today the state's ability to assure realization to a considerable extent of plan investment and production objectives has been described as depending upon only four means of intervention: subsidies, influence over loans negotiated by private parties, tax exemptions, and control of credit.[1] It would seem reasonable to add direct control of public investment to this list, a control exercised over an estimated 30 per cent of total investment in the French economy in 1963.[2]

EXTENT AND TYPE OF GOVERNMENT INFLUENCE ON INVESTMENT

The government has taken many actions with the advent of programming that have involved relatively small government expense. For example, it has changed laws formerly designed to discourage foreign investment, and it has begun a program of lowering tariffs, using this as a stick to coerce Irish industry into modernization and adaptation. The government has set up training facilities within the universities, through government agencies, and in private areas for increasing management abilities—perhaps one of the most crucial shortages from which Ireland is suffering. At small additional expense the government has injected momentum into agencies such as the Industrial Development Authority by supporting heartily their efforts to attract new foreign industry; it has expanded such agencies as *Coras Trachtala*, the Export Board, in order to increase contacts abroad and promote Irish exports; and it has worked closely with industry in setting up adaptation councils to advise and guide industries adjusting to conditions of freer trade. Government-industry consultations for reviewing and revising plan targets have been forums for examining ways to improve private industry performance.

While these actions may be described as necessary conditions for economic expansion along the paths designed by the Irish, they are not sufficient conditions for goal achievement. Contact and persuasion alone did not attract new foreign investment for the export sector needed under the program; the stick of lowered tariffs and the advice of consultants on modernization and adaptation did not provide the capital needed for adjustment to freer trade; and the provision of a growth perspective by the government did not leave the responsibility for increased industrial investment entirely with the private sector. Rather, investment by the government was channeled toward industrial output as opposed to social overhead capital; the stick of lowered tariffs was softened by the carrot of adaptation grants, and lenient credit to firms modernizing in the wake of freer trade; and foreign firms were enticed by grants and liberal credit, along with tax remission on exports.

Through these three types of government control and influence of investment—public investment by the government sector, credit control, and subsidies—implementation of plan goals became more a certainty and less a stated potential under "democratic" planning as adapted and applied by the Irish. Statistics are not available that would enable an accurate statement concerning the per cent of total industrial capital formation influenced by these implementation tools. Yet, it is informative to try to piece together a reasonable estimate. First, figures supplied by the Central Statistics Office of total gross domestic fixed capital formation financed by the state over the first six years of planning are used as a basis for estimating the amount of new *industrial* capital formation influenced or controlled by the government. To cross-check the first estimate, investment figures for 1958/59 are analyzed. Both approaches indicate the state has affected approximately three-fourths of new industrial investment in its efforts to achieve program goals.

The Central Statistics Office, replying to a question arising in the *Dail* (Parliament) on February 25, 1964, gave the following information for specified years on the amount of gross domestic fixed capital formation financed by the government.

TABLE 5

ANNUAL GROSS DOMESTIC FIXED CAPITAL FORMATION 1958-63
(£ million at current prices)

	1958	1959	1960	1961	1962	1963 (est.)
GDFC financed by public authorities	31.8	34.9	42.5	46.0	54.0	58.0
GDFC financed by statutory and semi-state bodies otherwise than from grants and loans by public authorities	12.2	9.9	8.5	9.3	15.0	23.0
GDFC financed otherwise	27.9	60.0	47.4	52.1	61.0	67.0
TOTAL GDFC	71.9	104.8	98.4	107.4	130.0	148.0

Source: Central Statistics Office.

The above table shows that slightly over half of gross capital formation since 1958 has been accounted for by the public sphere, partly financed by funds from the Exchequer and partly financed by the direct raising of capital on the market by state bodies. A glance at categories of investment represented by total gross capital formation reveals that the state probably accounted for at least half of industrial capital formation. All the categories used by the Central Statistics Office in breaking down gross fixed capital formation for submission to OECD, that is, agriculture, mining, manufacturing, construction, electricity, gas, water, transportation and communications, dwellings, public administration, and other service industries, reflect heavy influence of investment through state participation directly or indirectly. The other service category would include the state's participation in education and promotion of tourism, both through direct state investment and subsidies.

In addition to public investment the state stimulates considerable non-government investment. Of particular importance is the influence the state has had over new foreign investment by subsidies in the form of export tax remission of 100 per cent on profits from all new exports. As the next chapter will recount, export tax remission has been a major factor influencing new foreign investment in Ireland. Moreover, it is estimated that 85 per cent of the new private industrial capital investment from 1959 through 1963 is characterized by foreign participation. That is, £ 38.5 million of £ 45.4 million total industrial investment in new firms was accounted for by firms with foreign participation or firms wholly owned by foreign interests—the latter predominating when measured by pounds of new investment. [3]

Also, loans and grants by the government affect new investment. While they do not always finance completely the new investment, the availability of substantial state aid may be a prerequisite to investment. For instance, it was found that advice and persuasion were not sufficient to induce capital improvements needed by Irish industries if they were to adjust to conditions of freer trade. Therefore, in 1962 adaptation grants and special loans amounting to £ 3.8 million were approved by *An Foras Tionscal* (The Grant Board) for adaptation programs involving a total capital investment of over £ 20 million. [4]

Starting from the base of an estimated direct government investment of 50 per cent of new industrial investment, and adding to this the effect of government tax relief, grants, and credit programs, a conservative estimate would place government influence and control of investment as averaging over the past six years within the range of three-fourths of gross industrial investment.

An estimate of government domination of industrial investment in the year 1958/59 supports the above estimate that investment influenced by the government has been approximately three-fourths of gross industrial fixed capital formation. Using the figures that are available for the year 1958/59, and taking the same inclusive definition of "industrial investment" that was used above, the following table shows public capital expenditure by public enterprises:

TABLE 6

PUBLIC CAPITAL EXPENDITURE 1958/ 59
(£ million in current prices)

Ports, harbors, and airports	.91
Tourism	.02
Forestry (includes land acquisition)	1.14
Fisheries	.17
Fuel and Power	7.60
Telephones	1.45
Transportation	6.27
Industry	.54
TOTAL	18.10

Source: *Second Program for Economic Expansion,*
            Part II, p. 272.

Public investment accounted for approximately 38 per cent of total industrial investment in 1958/59. In 1959 there were approximately £ 14 million of new capital formation accounted for by new foreign industries that were eligible for 100 per cent tax relief on export profits. Many of these also received grants from the government. There is no way to calculate domestic investment influenced by grants, so this area of influence will be ignored, and it will be considered that large amounts of grants were received by foreign firms that also received subsidies in the form of tax relief.

The influence of the government over private investment in the form of credit accommodations should probably be included, however, in order to approximate more closely an accurate estimate of government repercussions upon new investment. The Industrial Credit Company, Limited, in its October, 1963, annual report states that in 1959 £ 1.8 million of capital in the form of capital underwriting, investments, loans, and hire-purchase activities were provided. It is assumed here that these loans gave rise to approximately twice that amount of fixed capital formation—a perhaps conservative estimate, but justified since a small percentage of this investment might have been included in one of the categories already accounted for.

The above calculations bring the total of fixed capital formation influenced by credit and subsidies to approximately £ 18 million, or approximately 38 per cent of the total industrial investment. Combining public enterprise investment with private investment influenced through subsidies and credit, it would appear that 76 per cent of total industrial investment estimated at £ 47.9 million in 1958/59 was controlled or influenced by state policy.

THE MIX OF IMPLEMENTATION TOOLS

Subsidies and direct government investment have been the two dominant tools used under the Irish expansion programs to influence industrial investment as outlined under the plans. Credit facilities, while vastly enlarged over pre-planning days, have occupied a lesser position within the mix of implementation tools. Among the subsidies designed to induce private industrial development along the lines laid down in the programs, tax relief has played the more prominent role, as the next chapter will show. Inasmuch as tax credit has been used largely in conjunction with grants, however, it is difficult to separate the effects of the two with precision. The mix of tools as it has developed was influenced by the goals of the programs and the four "C's" of "democratic" implementation techniques, as well as the early success of the various tools used to affect private investment. It is helpful at this point to discuss in more detail the Irish approach to selection of implementation tools to achieve goals of "democratic" planning.

GOVERNMENT ENTERPRISE AS AN IMPLEMENTATION TOOL

Government enterprise is quite compatible with the pragmatic approach to economic organization accepted by the Irish. Except for relatively mild political pronouncements by the Labor Party (a relatively weak political force on the current scene) no such dichotomy of ideas based upon the old conflict between socialist and laissez-faire ideology as evolved in England has hampered the use of public enterprise as a pragmatic instrument of economic accomplishment. And although the following statement is based upon observation rather than extensive research, it would seem that the more influential philosophical overtones shaping the approach to government enterprise are derived from the Catholic education in Ireland. A sense of the honor of public service and a concern for the welfare of the community as a whole, political, social, religious, and economic, have permeated the mental processes of the nation, and have resulted in the attraction to public service in the past of the more qualified minds of the nation. In this environment public enterprise has been accepted to the extent that it appears a likely instrument for furthering public welfare.

While there has been little if any pressure for nationalization resulting from adherence to ideological "isms," economic circumstances have brought about a pragmatic acceptance of the role of state enterprise in those areas of the economy where public enterprise can serve a worthwhile purpose in accord with current needs of the society, while not vitiating the general commitment to a market economy that is part of the political-economic heritage of Ireland. The development and growth of state activity is outlined by Garret FitzGerald as follows:

> ...some attempt must be made to explain the extent of state enterprise in Ireland and part at least of the explanation may be found in the economic circumstances of the new Irish State founded forty years ago. Owing to the difficult economic and social conditions in which the Irish State has had to operate, there has been, at least for much of the period in question, relatively little incentive for private enterprise to initiate certain activities which in other countries might be financially attractive. This has meant that, in order to speed up development, the state has had to intervene to establish and promote the expansion of particular industrial or commercial activities.

> The scale of state intervention required may have been intensified by the fact that, for historical reasons, even where development opportunities suitable for private enterprise have existed, the private sector in Ireland has in the past shown itself to be relatively unenterprising.[5]

The compatibility aspect of state enterprise is summed up by Dr. W. J. L. Ryan, head of Ireland's planning department, as follows:

...if history is any guide, there is no logical (nor, indeed, any inherent) limit in a democracy to the extent of state intervention in economic matters. The only limit is that imposed by public opinion and this relates to the methods by which the state should intervene.[6]

The broad basis for consensus concerning public enterprise in Ireland has enabled her to avoid such problems as England has experienced with changes in governments dedicated to opposing ideological pursuits in the economic sphere. Thus, Ireland has been fortunate in the respect that the compatibility of public enterprise with public opinion for the most part has resulted in a cooperative spirit for the country as a whole in the pragmatic division of labor between the public and private sectors within the over-all scheme for economic advancement.

Generally, public enterprise has been adjudged an expensive mode of assuring development goal attainments, and in fact was eventually abandoned to a large extent in Puerto Rico and Japan on this basis.[7] Also, the ability to control partially independent government enterprises so that national goals are achieved has proven to be as difficult in reality as it appeared simple in theory. This has bearing upon the fourth "C," conservation, or the degree to which an implementation tool conserves on government funds in relation to the success it achieves in the furthering of plan goals. Even in the absence of estimates on the amount of tax remission granted, it is probable that results in the form of new industrial development, specifically investment for the export sector, have been most expensive, pound for pound, when achieved through the instrument of public investment. This does not necessarily mean Ireland had or has a choice in this respect to a large degree, as will be discussed below; it simply points out the drain on public funds when public enterprise is used to achieve plan goals.

Of course some of the funds for public investment have come from profits earned by public enterprises and capital raised by bond flotations in the market. Of the £ 569 million of public capital expenditures projected for the period 1964/65 to 1969/70, it is expected that £ 163 million, or almost 30 per cent will come from internally generated funds of the state enterprises and the raising of capital on the market.[8] The state bodies have been interested in building up their own resources to the extent possible, especially since the capital shortage years of 1958/59 when funds were denied them. To the degree that they can provide their own funds they increase their independence. Of the major industrial trading bodies of the state, that is, the Sea Fisheries Board, Peat Production Board, Irish Sugar Company, Electricity Supply Board, Irish Steel Holdings, Limited, the Air Companies (*Aer Lingus Teo, Air Rianta Teo* and *Aerlinte Eireann Teo*), the new fertilizer company *(Nitrigin Eireann Teo)*, the telephone company, the transportation companies (including road, rail and water), and Irish Shipping, Limited, five were in a position to raise funds from internal and other sources in 1962/63.

TABLE 7

SOURCES OF FINANCE OF
FIVE INDUSTRIAL TRADING COMPANIES 1962/63
(£ millions)

Company	Total Expenditure	Public Funds	Internal Resources	Other sources e.g., banks insurance companies, etc.
Electricity Supply Board	9.75	.95	4.80	4.00
Irish Shipping, Limited	1.43	1.34	.09	
Peat Production Board	1.50	1.40		.10
Air Companies	1.01	.23	.55	.23
Irish Sugar Company	1.24	.56		.68

Source: *Budget 1963,* The Stationary Office, p. 50.

The provision of capital from sources other than public funds is rather recent in Ireland, starting in the 1950's and becoming accelerated with the shortage of public funds in 1958/59. Not all state bodies pay interest on public funds, although the Second Program states:

> So far as state-sponsored commercial and trading bodies are concerned...capital provided in future by the state will, as far as possible, take the form of loan capital on which, in the absence of specific and compelling reasons, interest will be payable by the state body. This will ensure that capital costs are taken into account in assessing proposals, will contribute towards moderating the growing cost of debt service...and encourage these bodies to look to non-Exchequer sources for their capital requirements.[9]

Currently there is not a shortage of capital in the Irish money market, and there probably would be a demand for share capital if state trading companies should offer stock to the public. The public was in fact invited to subscribe to shares early in the period of formation of state trading bodies, but the response was so poor that the idea was dropped. Overtures to the idea of reviving the offering of share capital to the public advanced in recent years (1960) by the Minister of Industry and Commerce, Mr. J. Lynch, were received with hostility by the Labor Party which felt it would lead to a decline in the level of government participation in the economy. It is far from clear, however, that such a possibility would be foregone in the future should the state desire to divest itself of interest in companies established, and use the money received in the sale of share capital to instigate new areas of state activity in line with development goals.

Also, the concept of mixed public-private trading companies is finding acceptance in Ireland, not so much as a positive instrument of government policy, as a necessary protection of state interests. Its development was traced in Chapter 4 as an outgrowth of the desire by the government to have some stake in firms receiving a large amount of public funds. The use of mixed public-private companies could improve the conservation aspect of state enterprise as an implementation tool to the extent that it would cut down on required capital without seriously diluting the control and direction of new investment in alignment with program goals.

The control of state investment by the planning authorities and Parliament is, in practice, not exceedingly strong. Among the more important reasons for this are the independence of centralized control established by the need for flexibility, and the independence sought by public enterprises, and encouraged by the government, through the obtaining of funds on the market for capital investment. Another important reason is the inability of the government control centers to review critically, and to challenge successfully, plans presented by the state companies in a country such as Ireland where there is an acute shortage of experienced managerial talent, and often the Board and/or Parliament are not sufficiently knowledgeable to evaluate actions of the public enterprises.

Thus, in practice there has been a good deal of independence in the operation of state enterprises, with the initiative coming from these state bodies, and the Board's role being one of very general supervision and co-ordination. Moreover, Parliament has not reviewed regularly the general policies (as opposed to day-to-day administrative policies which it leaves in the hands of the state enterprise) with any regularity or depth. A study done in 1954 on parliamentary control of the three largest public corporations in Ireland, the electricity, transport, and turf production companies, showed that the time spent on the affairs of the corporation by Parliament was small, and limited mostly to details and matters of local importance. [10]

Mixed public-private enterprises, as compared to wholly-owned public enterprises, might have much to offer in the conservation of public funds, while not seriously altering the extent of control by the planners. The pursuit of the general goal of productive investment has not involved, as yet, a strengthening of control over investment that would place the mixed enterprise in an inferior position in relation to controls needed for plan implementation. Rather, state funds devoted to mixed public-private companies would serve the same general purpose as public investment of a productive type—the purpose of increasing industrial activity. Moreover, to the extent that the mixture were one with foreign capital, domestic savings would be augmented and the marketing channels of foreign firms tapped, as well as foreign managerial ability.

This analysis is necessarily superficial to the extent that the fourth "C," conservation, implies efficiency in the use of state funds. There have been no depth studies of the efficiency of the state enterprises of Ireland and, of course, such a study would be subject to the difficulties involved in efficiency evaluations of state monopolies. [11] There is a general opinion by economists of Ireland that efficiency among the Irish public enterprises varies, and that a major shortcoming of most is in the area of marketing. A current marketing problem of note, because of its being the major example of public enterprise attempting to help goals of increased exports, is the effort by the Irish Sugar Company through its subsidiary, Erin Foods, to export processed food. While Erin Foods is considered an efficiently operated firm, it appears to have definite problems in the marketing field. The Irish airlines is an exception of note in that it has been very successful in marketing its products, and received international recognition for its advertising.

The efficiency of public enterprise as an implementation tool in general could not be based on Ireland's experience to date, however. Even if estimates of the efficiency of specific state enterprises were available, it would be difficult to generalize from such assessments the probable performance of new state enterprises in new lines of production. A myriad of different factors can affect enterprise performance. Thus, it would be hard to compare public enterprise efficiency with the return from state funds used in combination with private funds and private management, or to compare the results achieved through direct public investment with the return from state funds provided to entirely private business through grants.

Comments can be made for purposes of comparison, however, about conservation ratings in the use of public funds when those funds are used for tax remission as it is administered in Ireland. Under the state's remission of corporate profits taxes only the profitable firms are eligible, and the extent of tax remission varies directly with the amount of profits. Moreover, profits in the export field in Ireland are not likely to be dominated by monopoly profits since firms are competing in the international market and are not insulated from competition. The argument against tax remission is that it is allowed to the profitable firms that might otherwise contribute to socially remunerative public investment through tax payments. This argument may not be applicable, however, if the firms investing in a country would not have done so without the proffer of tax remissions. The findings in Chapter 6 indicate that new investment in Ireland in the export field would not have occurred in the volume needed to achieve a 7 per cent industrial growth rate without tax remission.

GOVERNMENT CREDIT AS AN IMPLEMENTATION TOOL

Credit has not played the dominant role under Irish planning that it did in the early years of French planning. The acute shortage of capital after World War II provided the Treasury with a built-in control mechanism in France. Access to the capital market was based upon contribution to the plan, and the Treasury was also empowered to give its guarantee to issues when the borrowing firms contributed to plan objectives. [12] Sheahan notes that the easing of the capital shortage in France has undermined to a considerable extent the power of credit control as a "persuasion" devise. [13]

A shortage of capital comparable to that in France did not exist in Ireland in 1958, and by 1964 the money market was highly liquid. The lack of a relative shortage in the capital area has led Irish planners to emphasize the positive aspect of general credit availability as a contributor to increasing over-all economic activity. This is different from the French approach to credit as an area for restrictive control to manipulate investment along the paths laid out in the plan. The contrast in the use of credit is also influenced by the fact that Irish planning has not reached the stage of detailed attention to investment areas that French planning has reached, and thus the plan sets no guidelines for alloting capital to specific industries. Rather, Irish investment goals are quite generally aimed at increasing over-all industrial activity. In addition, the role of credit as an implementation tool was reduced by the decision to give grants to firms expanding their industrial investment, and to new firms.

Nevertheless, the existence of a government agency that was accepted by the private economic community, and could support the plan goals through the encouragement of new private investment, resulted in funds being made available to the Industrial Credit Company in increased amounts with the advent of programming. Over one-half of the total capital provided by the Industrial Credit Company since its incorporation in 1933 has been provided since the inauguration of programming. [14] Gross loans in 1963 were £ 2.1 million as compared to an estimated average £ 2.4 million per year given in grants over the period of the First Program.

Thus, credit stimulus by the government was an accepted means of encouraging private investment in Ireland before the time of programming. The tendency in Ireland for private firms to finance internally, and the stagnant level of aggregate demand before 1959, meant that the Industrial Credit Company had scope for increasing its loans when the level of economic activity picked up, despite an increase in grants for long-term capital needs and working capital during the same period.

As currently administered in Ireland, government grants and government credit provide about the same degree of control over the direction of investment into areas desired by the planners. However, compared to grants, credit ranks higher in regard to conservation of state funds, even when it is given on terms that partly subsidize the borrower. Moreover, government guarantee of loans can encourage investment with less outlay of public funds than government grants or loans. Government guarantee of loans is effective so long as private capital market institutions are developed and funds are available for lending in the market. The Industrial Credit Company does not place its guarantee behind loans generally; however, it actively underwrites capital issues, agreeing to take up that portion of a flotation not subscribed to by the public, and then resells at a more propitious time.

The failure of credit facilities to play a more dominant role in the mix of investment implementation tools must be partly blamed upon the government's adherence to continuity and compatibility as guidelines for choosing their tools. By using an existing governmental agency to carry out credit needs under the plans, it relied upon a public financial company established in earlier years that had become, as is the tendency among so many financial institutions, a conservative, profit-making institution unwilling to assume above-average risks. The Industrial Credit Company is aware of the role a development bank could play in Ireland that actively sought to promote and encourage investment, despite an above-average risk, through lenient credit and even equity participations. However, it has so far leaned toward a passive role and profitable operations under the new expansion programs.

An exception is the large loans that have been extended at government direction to keep jobs open where private businesses that provided the main employment outlet for certain areas would have closed otherwise. The Industrial Credit Company has generally viewed these loans as a mar upon its record, and the government has now established a new agency to deal with such large loans where large risks are involved. The new arrangement (discussed in Chapter 4) could lead indirectly to mixed public-private firms inasmuch as an industrialist borrowing large sums from the government may substitute state equity for loan repayment.

SUBSIDIES AS AN IMPLEMENTATION TOOL

Subsidies in the forms of grants and tax remission have played a major role, along with government enterprise, in encouraging industrial investment, and have carried the major burden of stimulating investment in the crucial export sector (see Chapter 6). While no estimates are available on the amount of subsidies in the form of tax remission that have been received, the sum cannot be inconsiderable, and it mounts each year. Grants were increased dramatically starting in 1959 when it was decided to consider any new investment as highly eligible for grants so long as it contributed to program goals, whether it was in the areas designated as "undeveloped" or not. At the same time, increased funds were made available to *An Foras Tionscal,* the agency responsible for grants, with the result that, while grants as a form of subsidy were given to "undeveloped" areas of Ireland as early as 1952, 84 per cent of the total grants given were approved between April 1, 1959, and March 31, 1964. [15] As noted above, these grants averaged about £ 2.4 million per year over the First Program.

As in most economies, subsidies in one form or another have been in evidence in Ireland throughout its history. The tax remissions and grants, however, represent a new high level mark in the volume of direct subsidies received by business to encourage industrialization. Their existence might have been absorbed with little political repercussions or discussion in a country permeated by agricultural subsidies and used to the device, were it not for the fact that the prominent recipients of the subsidies have been foreign firms newly established in Ireland which are exporting approximately all of their production. This fact has resulted in a certain amount of resentment of subsidies as an implementation tool. Thus, while subsidies have possessed continuity and compatibility with the Irish economy and its reliance on an indirectly influenced private sector to achieve economic goals, they have not elicited a cooperative spirit as a whole on the domestic scene.

Direct grants in particular have met heavy criticism. They have gone to the same firms in large part that are also eligible for tax remission, that is, foreign firms. Moreover, direct grants for plant and machinery may go to firms that fail, whereas remission of profit taxes on exports goes to firms that are successful in their operations. The failure of firms that have received grants has intensified criticism of the grants as an implementation tool.

The pros and cons of tax remission versus direct grants are discussed in detail in Chapter 7. It is the general purpose of this section simply to point out that, in regard to cooperation and conservation, subsidies in the form of direct grants in Ireland cannot be ranked as highly as credit as an implementation tool. Moreover, as Chapter 7 points out, it is tax remission that is the dominant implementation device, not grants. The composition of the mix of implementation tools could be improved by revision of the role of direct grants. This, too, will be discussed in Chapter 7.

ASSESSMENT OF THE MIX OF IMPLEMENTATION TOOLS

The actual mix of implementation tools and the individual places of relative importance of particular types of tools within the mix were not completely controllable or predictable when planning was initiated in Ireland in 1958. It was natural, given the situation in Ireland in 1958, for the planning authority to rely on the channeling of public funds into industrial investment through the medium of state enterprises. In trying to attract foreign capital in the export sector, international examples and competition gave rise to the offering of grants and tax remission, and it would appear that the extent and size of these implementation tools were generally set to be lenient enough to attract foreign capital at a pace that could encourage rapid improvement in the economic situation. The use of industrial credit facilities was an extension of activities in existence, and, by making more funds available to the Industrial Credit Company, the government simply included this tool along with the others in the hope of encouraging industrial development to the maximum within the capacity of government action.

After six years of planning, the mix of implementation tools is dominated by the wholly-owned public enterprise and subsidies. At least three forces will have bearing upon the future mix within the Irish development endeavor: the large role that exports are assigned to play in the development plans, limitations upon the continued increase and dominance of the industrial sector by foreign capital, and limitations upon the continued expansion of public enterprise as an implementation tool.

Given the fact that Irish private enterprise does not have, and will not have for a while yet, the managerial know-how, technological advantages, or marketing channels that foreign capital can supply, it is highly desirable for foreign capital to continue to invest in Ireland. Yet, since the Irish are relying upon participant planning techniques of goal achievement, they are circumscribed by the limitations that foreign capital is placing upon the co-operative spirit of planning. In order for foreign capital to continue to be acceptable, it would appear that two changes in the mix of tools would be desirable.

First, in the future the negatively developed tool of mixed public-private enterprise might be changed into a positively designed technique for attracting foreign know-how and export ability in combination with government equity in cases where this would appear desirable. There would be several advantages to such an arrangement. It would avoid the financing of the whole project by the government where complete foreign ownership is undesirable. It would complement the Irish public enterprises in the area in which they have proven weakest—marketing for export. It would not drain public funds beyond capacity inasmuch as, with the increase in economic activity since the beginning of planning, shortage of capital has not been a crucial scarcity in Ireland. It would satisfy critics of foreign investment to the extent that the Irish would have an equity interest in the enterprise, and it would not greatly dilute control over the activities of the firm below the degree exercised over the relatively autonomous public enterprise in Ireland. Moreover, the mixed enterprise would avoid a major limitation upon the expansion of public enterprise into new fields—that is, the effect an increased role for the public enterprise would have upon the attraction of foreign capital. While wholly-owned public corporations tend to scare away foreign private investors, the mixed public-private company has many advantages for both the foreign private investor and the government.[16]

The second change in the mix of implementation tools that would appear desirable, given the framework of the Irish economy and the philosophy of planning that has been adopted, would be in the role of credit and grants. Assuming the findings of Chapter 6 to be reliable in establishing tax relief subsidies as the dominant attraction of foreign capital, it would appear desirable from the standpoint of increasing cooperation of the domestic business sector and developing domestic managerial talent, to concentrate grants and credit accomodations upon the goal of increasing the private industrial sector of the Irish economy. This would necessitate developing new criteria for allocation of grants and credit, and would demand a different approach to extension of credit, involving subsidizing new firms in part with low interest charges, and assuming risks more commensurate with those undertaken by development banks. The argument for an increased role for credit is presented in more detail in Chapter 7.

Whatever trend actually develops in the mix of implementation tools utilized in the achievement of program goals of industrial expansion in Ireland can have definite effects upon the pace and composition of industrial development. A continuation of the present trend could create an enclave of foreign firms that would expect to compete in the domestic market with the lowering of tariffs and entry into the European Economic Community. This could jeopardize the cooperation needed for "democratic" planning to succeed. If Ireland can avoid strong resentment of the foreign sector by the domestic business community, she stands to reap large gains from the contributions of foreign capital, while giving the domestic economy an environment within which to develop managerial talent and expand industrial activity.

Notes

1. Jean-Paul Delcourt, "Means by Which the State Can Influence Economic Development Under the Plan," *French and Other National Economic Plans for Growth,* Paris: The European Committee for Economic and Social Progress (CEPES), June, 1963, p. 24.

2. *Ibid.,* p. 32.

3. Industrial Development Authority sources.

4. *Second Program for Economic Expansion,* Part II, Dublin: Stationery Office, July, 1964, p. 149. This £ 20 million capital figure may include some working capital as well as plant, machinery, and equipment.

5. Garret FitzGerald, *State Sponsored Bodies,* Dublin: Institute of Public Administration, second edition (revised), 1963, p. 19.

6. *Investment Criteria in Ireland,* a paper read before the Society on November 17, 1961, Dublin: Cahill and Company, Limited, Parkgate Printing Works, p. 15.

7. See Thomas C. Smith, *Political Change and Industrialization in Japan: Government Enterprise, 1868-1880,* Stanford: Stanford University Press, 1955, and Milton C. Taylor, *Industrial Tax-Exemption in Puerto Rico,* Madison, Wisconsin: University of Wisconsin Press, 1957, *passim.*

8. *Second Program for Economic Expansion,* Part II, *op. cit.,* p. 274.

9. *Ibid.,* p. 240.

10. M. Scully, "Parliamentary Control of Public Corporations in Eire," *Public Administration,* XXXII (Winter, 1954), 455-62.

11. For a new approach to measuring productivity of government organizations, see *Measuring Productivity of Federal Government Organizations,* Washington, D.C.: U.S. Government Printing Office, 1964.

12. John and Anne-Marie Hackett, *Economic Planning in France,* London: George Allen and Unwin, Limited, 1963, pp. 265-268.

13. John Sheahan, *Promotion and Control of Industry in Postwar France,* Cambridge, Massachusetts: Harvard University Press, 1963, p. 181.

14. *Second Program for Economic Expansion,* Part II, *op. cit.,* p. 158.

15. *Ibid.,* p. 152.

16. Mexico, another country with a relatively stable government such as Ireland has, has succeeded in using the mixed public-private corporation to her advantage, and without the discouragement of foreign investment. See "Keeping Steam in Mexico's Boom," *Business Week,* November 28, 1964, pp. 90-97.

6 IMPORTANT FACTORS INFLUENCING NEW INVESTMENT IN IRELAND

How important a part did tax exemption, equipment grants, factory grants, and adaptation grants play in the dramatic increase Ireland witnessed in industrial expansion between 1958 and 1964? What factors other than tax exemption and grants played an important role in the 7 per cent annual industrial expansion over the life of the First Program? Why did 133 new firms with foreign participation representing a total investment of £ 38.5 million locate in Ireland during this period? Would they have come if there had been no government subsidies? Will they stay after expiration of the government subsidies? Answers to these questions were sought in interviews with top executives of 34 firms that had invested in new plant and equipment since 1957. Managing directors, assured that the information would not be identified with their firm, seldom hesitated in pin-pointing the important reasons for their investment.

COMMENTS UPON THE SAMPLE AND THE INTERVIEW

The population from which the sample was drawn was a list of 208 firms having new investment in plant and equipment above £ 2,000 during the first six years of planning. With the exception of firms receiving adaptation grants, a relatively small percentage of the total in terms of both number and pounds of new investment, the list was approximately complete. Government grants or tax exemption (and most often both) were received by almost all firms on the list. These subsidies were designed to achieve the program goal of greatly increased industrial investment, particularly new industrial investment in the export sector. Thus, new industrial investment was used as an indicator of goal success, and an interview sample was selected to test the importance of government tax exemption on export profits and government grants in achieving objectives for which they were designed.

A Random Sample

The sample of 34 firms was selected on a random basis from a population of 133 new firms with foreign participation, 55 new Irish firms, and 20 established firms with a large percentage of Irish ownership claims that had invested in new plant and equipment since 1957. Consideration was given to whether or not a stratified sample would be feasible, and increase the reliability of the data gathered. Among the *a priori* factors considered as being able to affect the role played by tax remission and grants in inducing new investment were:

1. Tax rates in the country of capital ownership, and existence of double taxation agreements between Ireland and the country of capital ownership.

2. Financial needs of the firm, i.e., need for subsidies.

3. Alternative sources of subsidies and their size.

A priori factors that might have affected location of foreign industry in Ireland, assuming firms would not locate in Ireland for tax reasons alone, include:

1. Factor combinations of the production process and their constancy, as well as the availability of different factors of production in Ireland in relation to the country of alternative location.

2. Transportation costs as a portion of production costs.

3. Proximity of markets and their size.

Stratification of the sample was rejected for several reasons: It would have been difficult and costly to obtain information necessary for stratifying the sample showing the exact impact of tax exemption by country on firms producing different products, and the financial needs of each firm. Moreover, cross-classification by all factors would have been unwieldly, while no small number of the above considerations present themselves as dominant factors that would yield a homogeneous grouping. Thus, a random sample was selected, and consideration was given to possible effects of the above type upon conclusions drawn from the data.

Tax rates in most countries of Europe, America, and Canada are generally high, and complete exemption is a considerable advantage. Thus, *a posteriori,* comments made by businessmen interviewed show stratification by taxes in the home country would not have influenced the data much, if at all. As is noted later, global information concerning the type of subsidies, size, drawing power, and extent of competition among various regions of the world giving subsidies would be valuable as background information for a study of this type.

Foreign Firms

The sample does not reflect nationality ownership claims in the population of firms having new investment in two respects. First, there are only 3 firms with German ownership in a sample containing 27 firms with foreign ownership, whereas the population contained German representation in 27 per cent of firms with foreign ownership claims. This bias resulted when interviews could not be arranged with high level executives of many German firms.

It is possible a larger inclusion of German firms would change the determinants of new investment, in that non-economic reasons may have influenced German firms to a greater degree than other foreign investors. Germans are not as welcome in Britain as in Ireland, and thus could choose Ireland as a route to the United Kingdom market that avoids location in Britain. Also, Germans have notoriously looked for *Lebensraum* away from Germany and the conflicts of the continent. Many Germans are purchasing land in Ireland. Economic factors would probably play a considerable part in the investment decision, however, and it is noteworthy that Germany has high corporate taxes and a tight labor market.

Second, American firms and firms with American ownership claims compose 44 per cent of firms with foreign ownership in the sample as opposed to 24 per cent in the population. A comparison of the replies of firms with American ownership to replies by other firms of the sample shows no marked difference in relation to determinants of new investment, importance of subsidies, geographic location, type of product, or markets.

Geographic Concentration

There have been two areas of heavy geographic concentration of new firms in Ireland since 1957—around the Dublin metropolitan area in the East, and in the vicinity of the Shannon Airport area in the West. The attraction of Dublin for new firms over the rest of Ireland is that of a relatively developed industrial complex with existing external economies and proximity to the United Kingdom market. There are higher subsidies at Shannon, plus duty-free entry and exit for those located at the Shannon Industrial Estate, which account in part for this area's attraction over other sectors of Ireland. It is surprising that Cork, Ireland's second largest city, located in the South near a big natural harbor, has not attracted a larger proportion of new firms than it has. One of the new oil refining firms is located near Cork to take advantage of shipping facilities.

The sample reflected the two areas of concentration in the population from which it was drawn. Concentration in these areas also reflected the fact that there were contacts available in Dublin and Shannon who were able to act as intermediaries in establishing interviews with executives who were involved in the investment decision. Approximately 45 per cent of new firms with foreign participation of the 133 in the population located in the Dublin area; the sample contained a 40 per cent representation for the Dublin area. The Shannon area attracted 20 per cent of new exporting firms with foreign participation. The sample was more heavily represented by firms in this area, showing a concentration of 35 per cent (i.e., two firms above the number that would make representation 20 per cent). Irish firms reflected the population distribution in that there was a concentration in the Dublin area and areas other than Shannon. The incidence of Irish ownership in the population was 35 per cent, that of the sample was 33 per cent.

Products manufactured by firms interviewed in the Shannon area were most often transportable by air, and produced by firms with foreign ownership. They were shipped to a more diversified array of markets than goods produced in the Dublin area. Firms in the East around Dublin had a higher proportion of their sales going to the home market than those in the West around Shannon. There was no particular geographic pattern reflecting type of product or labor intensive nature of the productive process.

Nine of the 12 firms located in the Shannon area were located at the Shannon Industrial Estate, 6 firms above the number that would have given a percentage representation reflective of the population. This is a possible source of bias in the sample, since the concentration could influence the reasons for new investment. Tax exemption is granted for 25 years at the Shannon Estate as opposed to 10 years outside of the Estate, and in certain cases grants have averaged above those given outside the Estate.

Firms in the sample not located at Shannon Estate mentioned tax exemption as being "important" or "very important" in 8 out of 10 interviews, while all firms at the Estate mentioned government subsidies as being of importance, and all but one listed them as "very important." However, the Shannon Estate firms differed very little from the other firms in their replies as to whether or not they would have invested without subsidies, and as to the incidence of interdependence of subsidies with other factors influencing new investment.

The concentration of firms at the Shannon Industrial Estate has probably increased the incidence of the "very important" listing in regard to subsidies, and the listing of government subsidies as "important" by about 3 per cent. The inclusion of 9 out of 15 manufacturing firms located at Shannon Estate gives an indication of the type of new investment at Shannon, its contribution to plan goals, and the reasons firms have located there.

Selection of Interviewee

In setting up interviews careful attention was given to contacting executives who were involved in the investment decision whenever possible. The fact that firms interviewed had all invested within six years prior to the interview, and most had invested within two years prior to the date they were canvassed, meant that personnel who were cognizant of the thinking and planning leading up to the investment decision were most often still with the firm.

Not all contacts were made through intermediaries, although roughly half were. In making direct contacts, names were obtained from the Export Board, the Department of Industry and Commerce, the Industrial Development Authority, and the Shannon Free Airport Development Company, Limited, of executives who were knowledgeable regarding the initial investment decision. These executives were written to directly. The letter contained identification of the interviewer, the purpose of the interview, the time required for the interview, assurance of confidential treatment of the information, and an introductory statement saying their firm was suggested as one of the firms with new investment in Ireland that had "outstanding management." Replies were generally prompt and favorable, some being forwarded to executives in Japan and America. Interviews were arranged in such cases when the executives were in Ireland next.

The Interview

The fear that foreign firms would not admit coming to Ireland because of the availability of subsidies there proved unimportant once executives were assured the information would not be identified with their firm. Executives were much more hesitant to admit "cheap labor" was a reason for investment than to say tax exemption was a determinant. This problem was anticipated and taken care of by listing "available labor" as well as "low-cost labor" upon the interview sheet as a category of investment determinants.

Irish executives of wholly-owned Irish firms often resented government subsidies as they are currently administered in Ireland. They were prone to criticize the subsidies, and try to avoid a discussion of their actual impact upon the investment decision. This reaction by Irish executives became apparent early in interviewing, and specific discussion of the importance of subsidies to the investment decision was elicited through more detailed questioning. In some cases more than one executive was interviewed and this helped to solidify answers.

Government Subsidies

Firms receiving adaptation grants and regular plant and equipment grants were, for the most part, firms that exported and were eligible for export profits tax remission. It was not possible to separate completely the role played by grants from that of tax exemption. Rather, it is noted that tax exemption was more often mentioned than grants; and it is suspected from comments made by executives that, had grants not been combined with tax exemption, grants would have had even less effect than the sample indicates, especially among foreign firms. Evidence also indicates the effect of tax exemption would not have been greatly reduced by the absence of grants among firms with foreign ownership.

There were few firms that did not mention government subsidies in reply to the question regarding important determinants of new investment. When subsidies were not mentioned during the discussion, then testimony as to their importance was asked for. The executive did not know that a primary purpose of the interview was to check on the effectiveness of subsidies. If government subsidies played an important part in the investment decision, executives were asked to rank them on a four-point scale. In doing this, they would sometimes go back and rank other factors named as influencing the investment decision on the top two points of the scale, distinguishing between those that were "important," and those that were "very important."

At least two Irish firms felt patriotic concern over Ireland's unemployment problem, and both said this concern was an impetus to investment. Two mentioned it as having "important" status as opposed to "very important." One mentioned low-cost labor as "important," and one placed "available labor" in this category.

DETERMINANTS OF NEW INVESTMENT

A summary of the findings in regard to major factors affecting new investment of the 34 firms interviewed is given in Table 8. The survey of 34 firms in the Republic of Ireland that invested during the first six years of planning indicates that subsidies, along with market demand and access conditions, have been the primary movers in the increase in private industrial investment over this period. The availability of labor ranked third in importance, and played an important role. No other factors mentioned approached the importance of these three reasons. Not surprisingly, raw material was mentioned only once.

In the absence of government subsidies it is possible that up to two-thirds of the new private investment in the industrial sphere in Ireland since planning began might not have taken place. Although not a *sine qua non* factor in every case, government subsidies carried weight in the investment decision in 85 per cent of the cases. Data collected indicate this figure would have been even higher if calculated as a percentage of pound investment influenced.

It would appear that in 34 per cent or more of the cases (depending upon the number giving "inconclusive" replies that would have invested in an actual situation where there were no subsidies) investment would have taken place without the subsidy program Ireland has initiated. The influence of grants, as opposed to tax exemption, was very low in this group of firms.

While 10 of the 34 firms did not give a direct "yes" or "no" response when asked "Would you have invested without government subsidies?" the replies

TABLE 8

IMPORTANT FACTORS INFLUENCING NEW INVESTMENT OF 34 FIRMS IN THE
REPUBLIC OF IRELAND 1958-64 (JULY)

	Very Imp.	Imp.	Of Little Imp.	Of No Imp.
1. Tax exemption on export sales	20	5	3	6
2. Equipment, adaptation, and factory grants	14	3	7	10
GOVERNMENT SUBSIDIES: CONSOLIDATED TOTAL	24	5		
3. a) Demand conditions in, and/or access to				
(i) United Kingdom market	13			
(ii) European market	4			
(iii) Protected Irish market	5			
b) Access to, and/or shipping point convenient to, world markets	9	1		
MARKET DEMAND AND ACCESS CONDITIONS: CONSOLIDATED TOTAL	22	1		
4. Available labor	14	1		
5. Low-cost labor	2	1		
LABOR: CONSOLIDATED TOTAL	14	1		
6. Provision of employment		2		
7. Need to cut costs and modernize because of recent lowering of tariff	2			
8. Duty-free import of raw material	2			
9. Industrial Credit Company funds	2			
10. Access to raw material	1			
11. Consultant grants	1			
12. Miscellaneous	3			

obtained from executives considering this hypothetical situation seem to carry weight for the importance of subsidies, especially where the firms could have located in another country that offered subsidies and/or had an available labor supply.

Seventy-one per cent of the business units firmly stated they expect to continue operations after expiration of the effect of the subsidies. Of course, this is a long look into an uncertain future, since Shannon tax exemption runs 25 years and tax exemption for firms located elsewhere does not end completely until 15 years from the date it is granted. At least, subsidy-attracted investment does not appear to admit to an impermanent nature. This is about all that can be said for this question and its responses.

In the allocation of equipment and other grants, Ireland has favored exporting firms. Tax exemption is available only on export sales. Thus, the fact that Ireland's new investment has been predominantly export oriented lends further evidence to the importance of her subsidy program. The data show the higher the percentage of sales that a firm exported, the more consistently did government subsidies play an important role in the investment decision. Moreover, of the firms exporting 30 per cent or more of their sales, only 22 per cent stated that they would have invested without government subsidies, compared to 34 per cent for the sample as a whole. There appears, then, to be strong evidence pointing to the importance of the role government subsidies are playing in the achievement of the program goal of increasing the exports of manufactured goods from Ireland.

While the United Kingdom market, with its custom-free access, is a boon to industrial location in Ireland, new investment is diversifying the ports of call for Ireland's export goods. Nine of the 22 firms locating because of reasons of markets were looking to world markets, with no one country heavily dominating their export field. Moreover, the condition of duty-free access to the United Kingdom market alone is not a sufficient reason for location in Ireland. Rather, firms selling a considerable portion of sales to the United Kingdom tend to come to Ireland for two additional reasons: the labor situation and government subsidies. And between the two, it is doubtful one plays a major role; rather the two seem to work in tandem. This suggests a differential in the Irish-United Kingdom labor markets of, among other possibilities, labor cost, availability, and aptitude. Thus, competition between Northern Ireland and the Republic of Ireland to attract new investment is not in subsidies offered alone, but in government subsidies *and* labor factors.

And in conclusion for the sample as a whole, firms investing because of market demand or access conditions found their decision depended upon the availability of government subsidies to a lesser extent than did firms investing in Ireland because of available labor. The trilogy, market-labor-subsidies, showed a great deal of interdependence of factor influence, and was, with the exception of one case, restricted to firms selling in the United Kingdom market.

A CLOSER LOOK AT THE DATA

Of the 20 firms listing tax exemption as "very important," 5 indicated they would have invested without government subsidy. Six of the 25 listing tax exemption as an important determinant of investment would have invested if there had been no tax exemption. Of the 17 firms listing grants under "important" and "very important" 3 would have invested without government subsidy.

By consolidating items one and two of Table 8, the following data emerge: Government subsidies were listed as "very important" by 24 of the 34 firms interviewed, or by 71 per cent. Government subsidies were given rankings of "important" or higher by 85 per cent, or 29 out of 34 firms. Of these 29 firms listing government influence as important, 8 stated they would have invested without government subsidies; 9 said they would not; 10 gave inconclusive answers; and 2 gave no reply. Of the same 29 firms, 21 expected to continue operations after expiration of the effects of government subsidies, 1 did not expect to continue, 5 gave inconclusive answers, and 2 gave no response. Of the 5 firms that failed to list any government subsidy as playing an important part in its new investment, 2 were British firms that located in Ireland before the policy of tariff reduction went into effect to get inside the tariff wall, and do not export; 1 exports 1 per cent of sales, 1 exports 15 per cent, and 1 exports 100 per cent, but located in Ireland for reason of agricultural raw material supply.

Two of the total sample of 34 firms are not representative of investment resulting from program policy, and their exclusion would add to the representativeness of the sample. These firms actually made their investment decision before announcement of the government's policy to lower tariffs progressively in preparation for entry into the Common Market, and as a spur to increased efficiency of home-manufactured goods. The 2 firms mentioned invested for the sole reason of supplying the Irish market, which was, at the time of investment, protected by a rather high tariff wall or quota system on the goods they produced.

Excluding these 2 firms, and using a base of 32, then 75 per cent of the firms investing since 1957 listed government subsidies as "very important." Eleven of these 32 firms would have invested without any government subsidy. That is, in 34 per cent of the cases where the government dispensed equipment grants, for example, or allowed profits on exports to go tax-free, the executive interviewed firmly stated that investment would have been made without the prospect of tax exemption or other subsidies offered. It should be noted, however, that 8 of the 11 firms that said they would have invested without government subsidies, also said that government subsidies were an "important" or "very important" factor influencing their decision to invest.

Ten firms gave inconclusive replies to the question "Would you have invested without government subsidy?" finding it hard to reply positively to a hypothetical situation with which they were not actually confronted. In looking at the influence of government subsidies as suggested by results of the questionnaire, two questions emerge at this point. First, is there reason to doubt the truthfulness of the "yes" and "no" answers to the above question; and second, how should the inconclusive answers be weighed and interpreted?

In answer to the first question, the following impressions and arguments lend credence to the accuracy of both the "yes" and "no" replies. Location because of subsidy alone, or predominantly, is often considered to carry with it implications of doubt as to the efficiency or respectability of the firm. Evidence of this feeling was prevalent in Ireland, but it is felt that the confidential status of the interview contributed to the response of the 9 firms that said they would not have invested without government subsidy.

The possibility remains, however, that those replying "yes" were partly intimidated by prevalent attitudes toward subsidies despite the confidential status of the questionaire. Yet, the 11 answers of "yes" appeared to be consistent with replies to other questions on the interview form (the question on subsidies was always asked last), and to be uttered firmly enough in each case to place reliance on the responses. For example, labor was mentioned as an over-riding need in several cases; and one company came to Ireland because there would have been higher tariffs imposed by Commonwealth nations on its goods if they had been manufactured in the firm's home country and shipped to Commonwealth countries. In other cases, market or cost savings made investment profitable without tax exemption. Similar cross-checks on the 9 "no" answers support their reliability.

It is doubtful that the 10 inconclusive answers reflect a 50-50 probability of going either way. There are at least three reasons for this conclusion. First, firms giving inconclusive answers could very easily be susceptible to the popular thinking referred to above that there is a taint of irrespectability connected with subsidies, and furthermore, that a firm locating in response to subsidy attractions alone is a financially weak or inefficient operation. Secondly, the comments made in answering the question "Would you have invested without government subsidy?" seem to reflect an uncertainty closer to a "no" answer than to a positive opinion. These comments are as follows:

1. Hard to say. Tax exemption, not other subsidies, is the important consideration. Looked into tax exemption other places (Bahamas) but location was important because of liason between this company and the parent company in England. Thus, the Bahamas were not so attractive.

2. No, if no assistance at all, because they offered some help in Northern Ireland.

3. Might have, because it would have been more expensive to expand

in London. Most important were the factory outlay and smooth supply of labor. Would have had to go fifty to eighty miles out from London. Northern Ireland came late and offered less.

4. Possibly—looking for distribution center.

5. Would have been loathe to make such an expensive investment at this time in export equipment because there is a great deal of risk in the export market.

6. Spain and Portugal were considered along with Ireland. Ireland was chosen because of grants and better quality labor than Spain or Portugal.

7. Would have taken one big advantage away. Would have had to consider closely.

8. Yes, now; but don't know if would have at the time.

9. Would have gone out of Germany to get labor. The United Kingdom considered, but a German company would not be so well received there.

10. Very hard to say. Perhaps with loss of both tax exemption and grants answer would be no; with loss of only one, yes.

Thirdly, the Republic of Ireland was competing with other countries in the giving of concessions in at least 5 out of the 10 cases (Numbers 1, 2, 3, 6, and 9) where inconclusive answers were given. In retrospect, it would have been advantageous to have asked each firm if any other location than Ireland was seriously considered in order to get an idea of how much firms shop around, and of the international competitiveness in the subsidy market. This question was asked indirectly where a firm listed, for example, the United Kingdom market as playing a key role in its decision to invest in Ireland, but did not list tax or other subsidies as an important factor in their investment decision. In such cases the executive interviewed was asked why the firm did not locate in the United Kingdom; and if labor was mentioned as a reason where there was a United Kingdom market, but government subsidies were not mentioned, the possibility of locating in parts of the United Kingdom where there is surplus labor (e.g., Northern Ireland) was mentioned to elicit comments on the competitiveness of the two areas in regard to surplus labor and subsidies.

It would seem from the comments that were made during the interviews that the Republic of Ireland is competing with the United Kingdom (especially Northern Ireland),[1] as well as other countries and sub-areas of countries where subsidies are offered by governments trying to encourage investment, and where surplus labor is available. Competition is undoubtedly heightened by the fact that Ireland is in part attracting business units specializing in light manufacturing and processing, whose goods are often transportable by air, and whose markets include several countries around the world. These units can economically locate in a number of areas, and as a result, tend to pay close attention to such barriers or advantages in the international trade field as customs duties, tariffs, trade agreements, and subsidies. Support for this conclusion also emerges in further analysis of data that follow.

Of the 34-firm sample, 26 export more than 29 per cent of annual sales, and 22 export 50 per cent or more, testifying to the fact that the largest part of Ireland's new investment has been in the export field where tax exemption is allowed. Of the 26 firms exporting 29 per cent or more of their sales, 23 (90 per cent) listed government subsidies as "very important," and 25 of the 26 ranked government subsidies important or better. The one that did not mention tax subsidies in the important category was the one firm in the sample that gave raw material as an important reason for location in Ireland. Six of the 26 firms, or 22 per cent, stated that they would have invested without government subsidies.

Nine of the 34 firms were located in the Shannon Industrial Estate where tax exemption on export sales is granted for 25 years, as compared to 10 years of tax relief in other parts of Ireland. All 34 firms listed government subsidies as important, and all but one listed them as very important. Yet, the Shannon firms adhered closely to the distribution for the sample as a whole: in 3 cases investment would have taken place without government subsidies; in 2 cases no investment would have taken place without subsidies; and in 4 cases the replies were indecisive. Of course, the Shannon sample was necessarily a small one, since there are only 15 manufacturing firms located at the Shannon Industrial Estate, and one firm can change the percentage disproportionately in a small sample.

All of the Shannon firms were queried in regard to the effect European Economic Community membership by Ireland would have upon their operations at Shannon in light of the fact that there were many comments among businessmen and government officials in Ireland indicating concern that if European Economic Community membership were obtained, Shannon would "fold up." None of the 9 Shannon firms interviewed out of the total of 15 firms at the Estate saw European Economic Community entry as jeopardizing their operations. Seven said it would help their business, 1 said it would make no difference, and 1 had not studied the possibility carefully.

Of the 13 firms listing demand conditions in and/or access to the United Kingdom market as a "very important" reason for investing, 6 listed labor and government subsidy along with the United Kingdom market as important reasons influencing their decision. Of these 6, 5 sold more than 15 per cent of their goods to the United Kingdom, whereas of the 7 listing the United Kingdom market, but not mentioning labor as an influencing factor, 5 had less than 16 per cent of sales going to the United Kingdom. Of these 13 firms, the distribution in reply to the question of whether they would have invested in the absence of government subsidies does not vary markedly from the sample of 34 firms interviewed. Three of the 13 firms would not have invested without government subsidies, 5 would have (only 1 of these 5 had a major market in the United Kingdom), and 5 gave inconclusive answers.

Item number 3, Market Demand and Access Conditions, has been broken down to show what markets are playing dominant roles in reasons for locating in Ireland. Where world markets were mentioned as an important factor in choosing a location point, breakdowns of these markets showed the United Kingdom mentioned the greatest number of times as receiving 10 per cent or more of export sales, while European markets were among the markets receiving 10 per cent or more of sales in three cases. Only 1 firm mentioned the European market alone as a major reason for new investment, although many firms that located in Ireland primarily because of available labor shipped to the European market. For the sample as a whole, there were 2 firms shipping to the United Kingdom for every 1 shipping to Europe. Two of the 5 firms listing the protected Irish market in their replies to the questionnaire invested before the lowering of tariffs became a government policy.

All but one of the firms listing available labor as "important" or "very important" listed government subsidies among the important reasons for their new investment in Ireland. Although low-cost labor was mentioned only two times, a large number of firms employed a large percentage of female workers who can legally be paid less than male workers in Ireland. It is highly likely that low-cost labor played a much larger role than admitted by interviewees, but that the opprobrium associated with "exploitation of labor" helped to translate "low-cost labor" into "available labor" in the executive's vocabulary. [2]

Item number 7, modernization resulting from the lowering of the tariff, should not be viewed as reflecting representation of this reason in the sample. Six established or "old" firms having partial or complete Irish ownership were interviewed. These firms were mentioned by Irish contacts as having new investment, and possibly adaptation grants. The government will not release names of those firms receiving adaptation grants until the completion of the distribution of grant funds. It is undoubtedly too early yet to assess fully the effect of the government's carrot and stick policy of lowering tariffs, while holding out the offer of adaptation grants for modernization and rationalization investment to help firms compete under freer trade conditions.

The sample shows that government subsidies, market and available labor dominated the causal factors influencing new investment over the past six years in Ireland. Their interdependence is evidenced as follows: 13 of 34 firms list labor together with government subsidy as "very important." Three of this group would have invested without government subsidy according to their questionnaire replies. Fourteen of 34 firms list market together with government subsidy as "very important." Of the 23 firms listing market as important, 17 listed government subsidies as "important" or "very important." Of this 17, 5 said they would have invested without government subsidies. Seven firms from the sample list market, labor, and government subsidy together as important determinants of new investment; 8 list market and labor together.

INVESTMENT IN THE ABSENCE OF SUBSIDIES

The question "Would you have invested without government subsidies?" was designed to isolate more firmly the importance of government subsidies than was divulged by the ranking of government subsidies along a scale of importance. Replies to this question break the sample down into three groups: those that would have invested without government subsidies, those that would not have, and those that gave inconclusive answers. Certain patterns can be discerned among the three groups that throw light upon the importance of government subsidies in industrial investment as well as the characteristics of government-influenced investment.

Four firms are left out of the following tables. Two invested before the government's tariff-reducing policy, and 2 gave no reply to the above question. Data from the interview questionnaire are listed for the remaining 30 firms with the exception of ownership by country and industry. The three-group breakdown showed no pattern by ownership or industry, and this information is withheld to avoid identification of firms that have cooperated in giving confidential information. Comments explaining and amplifying the tables follow each table. These comments are numbered in order to facilitate comparison of similar comments upon all three tables.

Before summarizing and drawing conclusions from the grouped data, it should be noted that the annual sales figures in a large number of cases did not reflect a run at full production for the last year because many firms were relatively new. Employment figures do not suffer as much from this shortcoming as they were given as of the day of the interview. Sales figures have been listed, but because of the foregoing reason, they are referred to cautiously in making comparisons among the three firms, and cannot be interpreted as being as good an indicator of the contribution of the firm to the economy as investment figures.

Omitting the cases where data were not available, firms that stated conclusively they would have invested without government subsidies invested, on the average, £ 136,000 per firm less than firms that stated they would not have, and £ 254,000 less than those firms that gave inconclusive answers. The latter firms invested, on the average, the largest amount in plant and equipment of the three groups.

Omitting the old, established firms from the average, the group that would have invested even though subsidies were not forthcoming employed an average of 200 employees, while the groups giving a "no" or "inconclusive" answer to the question "Would you have invested without government subsidies?" employed an average of 106 and 223 employees per business unit respectively, making an average of 165 employees per firm for the latter groups combined.

In absolute terms, then, the group that would have invested without government subsidies employed more people per business unit than the other

TABLE 9

ELEVEN FIRMS THAT WOULD HAVE INVESTED WITHOUT GOVERNMENT SUBSIDIES

Factors Influencing Investment and Related Data

Important Factors Influencing Investment

	Total	Firm Number										
		1	2	3	4	5	6	7	8	9	10	11
Government grant very important	2							X				X
Tax exemption very important	5	X	X	X	X	X						
Government subsidy important	8	X	X	X	X	X	X	X	X			
Labor	4	X		X	X		X					
Market	8		X	X		X	X	X		X	X	X
Raw material	1									X		
Modernization	1							X				
Other	2	X							X			

Investment in Plant and Equipment and Other Related Data

	Average	1	2	3	4	5	6	7	8	9	10	11
Investment in plant and equipment since January, 1958 (million pounds)	.242	1.+	.24	.185	.286	.125	.075	.25	.012	na	.006	na
Annual sales (million pounds)	.967	4.5	.05	na	1.1	.3	.1	1.5	.025	na	.13	1.0
Per cent of sales exported	53	30	15	100	100	100	10	10	100	100	15	negl.
Number of employees	200	850	32	80	500+	110	45	(800)	25	75	(40)	85

COMMENTARY ON TABLE 9

1. Two of the 11 firms are old, established firms that are expanding or modernizing, and the number of employees and annual sales listed for these two firms are for the entire operations.

2. Omitting the old firms (Numbers 7 and 10) and firm Number 9, which is just starting operations and could not give complete information, the remaining 7 firms showed an average investment to employment ratio of .276/235.

3. Six of the 11 firms export less than 31 per cent of sales; 5 export less than 16 per cent.

4. Government grants were listed as important by only 3 firms, of which 2 listed them as "very important." Six listed tax exemption as important, 5 of these listing it as "very important."

5. Of the eight firms listing market as an important factor, 4 sold approximately 10 per cent of their sales to the United Kingdom; 1 firm, Number 3, sold 80 per cent of sales to the United Kingdom.

TABLE 10

NINE FIRMS THAT WOULD NOT HAVE INVESTED WITHOUT GOVERNMENT SUBSIDIES

Factors Influencing Investment and Related Data

Important Factors Influencing Investment	Total	Firm Number								
		1	2	3	4	5	6	7	8	9
Government grant very important	7		X	X	X	X		X	X	X
Tax exemption very important	7	X			X	X	X	X	X	X
Government subsidy important	9	X	X	X	X	X	X	X	X	X
Labor	3						X	X	X	
Market	4	X	X						X	X
Duty-free import of raw material	1	X								
Recent lowering of tariff	1			X						
Industrial Credit Company funds	1			X						

Investment in Plant and Equipment and Other Related Data

	Average	1	2	3	4	5	6	7	8	9
Investment in plant and equipment since January, 1958 (million pounds)	.378	.18	.6	.9	.25	.075	.1	.05	1.2	.05
Annual sales (million pounds)	1.026	.085	4.5	.5	.5	.5	.25	*	.85	na
Per cent of sales exported	72	100	50	40	40	100	50	100	96	large
Number of employees	106	20	(1500)	(270)	(1200)	120	80	60	250	na

*Production goes to parent company

COMMENTARY ON TABLE 10

1. Three of the 9 firms are old, established firms that are expanding or modernizing and the number of employees and annual sales listed for these 3 firms are for the entire operations.

2. Omitting the old firms (Numbers 2, 3 and 4) and firm Number 9 which is currently under construction, the remaining 5 firms show an average investment to employment ratio of .321/106.

3. None of the firms export less than 40 per cent of sales.

4. Five listed both government grants and tax exemption as "very important." The remaining 4 listed one of the two as "very important." Government subsidies were the only important reasons for investing in 2 cases.

5. Two of the 4 firms listing market as an important reason for investment named the United Kingdom market where they sold 40-50 per cent of their goods.

TABLE 11

TEN FIRMS GIVING INCONCLUSIVE REPLIES IN REGARD TO INVESTMENT WITHOUT GOVERNMENT SUBSIDIES

Factors Influencing Investment and Related Data

Important Factors Influencing Investment	Total	Firm Number									
		1	2	3	4	5	6	7	8	9	10
Government grant very important	6	X	X	X		X	X	X			
Tax exemption very important	7		X	X	X	X	X	X	X		
Government subsidy important	10	X	X	X	X	X	X	X	X	X	X
Labor	7	X	X	X			X	X	X	X	X
Market	8	X		X	X	X	X	X		X	X
Duty-free import of raw material	1									X	
Industrial Credit Company funds	1					X					
Other	2		X						X		

Investment in Plant and Equipment and Other Related Data

	Average	1	2	3	4	5	6	7	8	9	10
Investment in plant and equipment since January, 1958 (million pounds)	.496	1.0	.3	na	.75	.825	.1	.3	.714	.475	0*
Annual sales (million pounds)	2.165	na	.025	na	8.3	7.0	.2	.3	.893	.5	.1
Per cent of sales exported	93	75	99	100	100	60	100	100	100	100	100
Number of employees	223	160	85	600	160	(1000)	160	97	480	170	101

*Uses rental equipment

COMMENTARY ON TABLE 11

1. One of the 10 firms is an old, established firm that is expanding and modernizing and the thousand employees and annual sales for this firm are for the entire operation.

2. Omitting the old firm (Number 5) and firm Number 3 where figures are unavailable, the remaining 8 firms have an average investment to employment ratio of .342/177.

3. All of the firms are extremely heavily committed to export markets.

4. A majority of the firms (8) were influenced by more than two factors. Half of the 10 firms listed labor, market, and government subsidy together as important reasons for investment. Eight of the firms listed government subsidies as "very important," and all included it as a factor of importance.

5. Of the 8 firms listing market among important influencing factors, 5 ship to the United Kingdom, and 4 have major markets in the United Kingdom, shipping more than 50 per cent of sales to that region.

firms of the sample, and invested less capital per firm than the groups giving "no" or "inconclusive" answers.

A comparison of capital intensity ratios shows that the group that felt government subsidies were not so important as to prevent their investing, was more labor intensive than either of the other two groups. Capital/labor ratios were computed for those new firms giving figures for both. The capital/labor ratio for those 7 firms that would have invested in a situation where no government subsidies were offered was 276/235; for the 5 new firms that would not have invested in such a situation the ratio was 321/106; for those 8 new firms that could not conclude exactly what results a situation of no subsidies would have produced, the ratio was 342/177.

It should be noted that the electrical industry employs 1,462 of a total of 1,802 employees in the group that is relatively labor intensive. Without the three electrical firms, the average employment per firm would drop drastically from an average of 200 workers per firm to an average of 58 workers per firm. The only other electrical firm in the sample is in the group of 10 firms giving inconclusive replies. It accounts for the highest employment figure among the 9 new firms in this group.

The group of 11 firms that would have invested without subsidies contains all of the 5 firms in the three-group sample that export less than 16 per cent of sales. This group shows an average of 53 per cent of sales exported, compared to 72 per cent for firms giving a "no" answer and 93 per cent for firms giving inconclusive replies. It is safe to say this group exporting 53 per cent of sales is contributing less than the other two groups to exports, since its sales volume is lower than that of the other two groups.

Exports went to the United Kingdom more frequently than to any other market. Of the firms naming market as an important factor influencing their investment decision, those that shipped over 40 per cent of their sales to the United Kingdom tended to be in the "inconclusive" or "no" groupings; while of those shipping 10 per cent to 15 per cent of their sales to the United Kingdom, most said they would have invested without government subsidies. Labor was mentioned by all but one of the firms exporting over 40 per cent of their sales to the United Kingdom. In contrast, labor usually did not play a part in the investment decision of firms exporting 10 per cent to 15 per cent of their sales to the United Kingdom, although government subsidies were mentioned by these firms without fail. Of the 5 firms in this latter group, 3 had Irish capital and a domestic market.

Grants were mentioned much less often, and tax exemption was mentioned approximately half as many times, by firms that said they would have invested without government subsidies, as compared to firms that would not have, or gave inconclusive answers.

It is informative to rearrange the above data by groups in order to summarize the nature of the two groups where influence by government subsidies was strongest, and the nature of the group where it was weakest, although not unfelt.

Firms that would have invested without government subsidies were not relatively large firms on the average, measured either by capital investment or sales, although the electrical firms did not contribute to this size deficiency. They were firms that tended to give more employment per pound invested than other groups, however. Yet, market demand or access conditions were determinants of investment in twice as many cases as labor. Although 5 of the 8 firms in this group listing market as an important factor sold to the United Kingdom market, only 1 sold a major percentage of sales there, and the United Kingdom was only one of other markets influencing the investment decision in most cases. This group of firms truly presents a set of paradoxes:

1. Labor is mentioned only half as often as a major factor as are government subsidies and markets, yet this group of firms is relatively labor intensive.

2. Markets are mentioned 8 out of 11 times, yet this group exports the lowest percentage of sales of any of the three groups.

3. Government subsidies are mentioned 5 times along with only one other causal factor, yet these firms stated they would have invested without government subsidies.

However, out of the contradictory nature of this group come a few generalizations that give insights into the nature of these business units. Firms that said they would have invested without government subsidies,

1. often had a stake in the home market as well as export markets.

2. attached little importance to subsidies in the form of grants.

3. exported a lower percentage of their sales than the other firms in the sample and hence found tax exemption on exports less important than the other firms.

4. numbered among their group 3 electrical industry firms that were the main contributors to the labor intensive status of the group, and located for reasons of labor in 2 of the 3 cases.

5. contributed less to the economy in terms of pounds invested in plant and equipment, and in terms of export sales, than the other two groups.

In contrast to the above group is the group of 9 firms that stated they would not have invested had government subsidies not been offered to them. Besides their dependence on government subsidies, the firms in this group,

1. possessed the most capital intensive firms in the sample, measured in terms of capital/labor ratios.

2. contained the only two cases where government subsidies were named

as the only important factor influencing the investment decision.

3. is the smallest group of the three but, as discussed earlier, probably can number among its numbers many of the firms that gave inconclusive answers.

4. contained the one firm that stated conclusively it does not intend to continue operations after expiration of the subsidies.

5. contributed markedly less to employment on the average for new firms than did the new firms in the "yes" group.

6. exported, on the average, 72 per cent of their sales. This figure rises to 88 per cent when calculated on new firms only, omitting the 3 old, established firms that showed a higher concentration in this group than in other groups.

The final group, the group of 10 firms giving inconclusive replies,

1. made the largest contribution of the three groups to economic activity measured in terms of new investment.

2. made the largest contribution to exports.

3. unanimously listed government subsidies as playing a role in the investment decision.

4. made an important contribution to employment on a per-new-firm basis, although not as high a contribution as the "yes" group.

5. showed, among those firms listing market as an investment-determining factor, the largest number of business units with major markets in the United Kingdom.

6. had a predominance of firms that listed more than two factors as influencing the investment decision (most often labor, market, and government subsidies), which probably contributed to their inconclusive replies to the hypothetical question "Would you have invested without government subsidies?"

In interpreting the results of the three-group comparison it is obvious that the smallness of the groups means that the addition or deletion of two or three firms from any of the three groups could change the picture substantially. For this reason, averages have been interpreted cautiously, and components of the groups examined, where characteristics of individual firms have influenced the composition of the averages so as to present a misleading picture of a heterogenous group. Despite the limitations of the sample, important insights have emerged. The next chapter will use some of these conclusions in analyzing the use of government subsidies in Ireland to implement program goals.

From the sample breakdown, however, emerges a conclusion possessing a high degree of reliability, and reinforcing the answer found earlier (from examination of the sample data as a whole) to the crucial question of this chapter: How important a part have government subsidies played in the dramatic increase Ireland has witnessed in industrial expansion over the past five years, as compared with her economy's previous performance in this sphere? The foregoing breakdown of the sample points up the fact that firms highly influenced by government subsidies, that is, those that would not have invested without them or gave inconclusive answers, contributed more to the economy in terms of investment, sales, and exports than the group of firms that found subsidies relatively unimportant. And while firms that would have invested without government subsidies employed a larger number of workers per firm on the average, there were only 11 such firms compared to 19 firms where government subsidies were more important. Thus, new firms in the latter group provided 741 more jobs for the economy than the labor-intensive group. Without government subsidies industrial investment, exports, and employment would have been well below the levels achieved over the past six years, even though some members of the "inconclusive" group might have invested in the absence of subsidies. For a nation finding imperative reasons for industrializing and increasing exports within a limited time period, and having a need to lay access to the gains and momentum emanating from large doses of concerted investment, this is a conclusion of vital significance.

CLASSIFICATION BY PRODUCT

As the following table shows, government subsidies have been important determinants of new investment for the great majority of product categories of the sample. The products reflect the diversity found in the population from which the sample was drawn.

The miscellaneous category includes umbrellas, floor maintenance equipment, greeting cards, spectacle frames and sunglasses, industrial diamonds, paint brushes, adhesive tape, and fork-lift trucks. Most of the products listed in Table 12 are exported, and are easily transported at a relatively low cost.

While labor is an important attraction for new firms, more important seems to be the attraction of subsidies in a country located close enough to Europe's expanding markets to enable profitable export operations.

The products as categorized in Table 12 did not exhibit any pattern by country of ownership interests. Foreign market outlets reflected the lessening of complete dependence upon the United Kingdom market outlined in Chapter 2. Most goods are shipped to Europe and America, with no particular concentration by product.

The availability of labor was not always listed as a determinant of new investment in the relatively labor intensive industries. In the categories of clothing, carpets, textiles, and food products, there were a number of established firms desirous of increasing exports, and these listed government subsidies and markets as the determining factors. The electrical and electronic products category includes some products that are produced by a relatively labor intensive process, and some products that require less labor. This may account for labor not being listed in two out of four cases there.

The product category contributing more new pounds of investment than any other category was the rather inclusive one of metal and metal products. This category involves such diverse products as cutting tools, heaters, precision fasteners, and pots and pans, and contributed £ 2.3 million to new investment. Second in total contribution by pounds to new investment was electrical and electronic products (£ 2 million); third was clothing, carpets, and textiles (£ 1.4 million); and fourth was food products (£ .97 million).

Several product groups listed involve a large enough number of firms to get an idea of capital investment patterns. For example, electrical and electronic products accounted for the largest per firm investment in new plant

TABLE 12

IMPORTANT FACTORS INFLUENCING NEW INVESTMENT BY PRODUCTS

Product Category	No. of Firms	Government Subsidies	Markets	Labor
Clothing, carpets, and textiles	6	6	2	4
Metal and metal products	5	5	5	3
Electrical and electronic products	4	4	2	2
Food products	3	2	3	1
Pharmaceuticals	2	2	1	
Chemicals	2	1	2	
Data services and products	2	1	2	1
Paper and paper products	1	1		
Plastics	1	1	1	
Miscellaneous	8	6	5	4

and equipment (£ 502,750), with metal and metal products ranking second (£ 460,500). Interestingly, electronic and electrical firms also contributed more than most other areas to enlarged employment opportunities in manufacturing. Average investment per firm in food products was £ 321,667, while that of clothing, carpets and textiles was £ 281,200. The latter was below the average investment per firm of £ 293,333 for the miscellaneous category.

The United Kingdom market was listed more often as an export market among firms producing food products and clothing, carpets, and textiles than in the other categories accounting for large increases in investment. The two categories together showed a higher incidence of Irish ownership and production for the home market than other product areas, although the major goal of new investment was to increase exports and/or modernize in order to stay competitive under conditions of freer trade. Both categories have been areas of traditional business activity in the Irish economy.

The sample indicates government subsidies have been instrumental in stimulating new industrial investment in a range of products, many new to the Irish economy, and that diversification of production goods and export markets have occurred together. Among the product categories of the sample, the electrical and electronic category stands out as having made large contributions to at least three goals—increased employment, increased industrial investment, and increased export markets. Government subsidies were an important determinant of new investment for all firms interviewed in this category.

Notes

1. An advertisement in a U.S. magazine reads: "U.S. managements state that their reasons for selecting Northern Ireland for overseas production are based on three fundamental considerations—Government assistance and co-operation, labor conditions, and market accessibility." *Business Week,* New York: McGraw-Hill, Inc., March 14, 1964, p. 127.

2. Wage rates normally run $29.50 to $36.50 per week for skilled adult men, and $23.60 to $29.50 for unskilled and semiskilled; skilled women receive $15-$20 and unskilled $12-$17. There is a 40-45 hour work week.

CHAPTER 7 A PARTIAL ANALYSIS
OF THE USE OF SUBSIDIES
IN THE IRISH ECONOMY

Resentment over the presence of foreign capital and the use of subsidies as a way of increasing industrial activity is not uncommon in Ireland. And there is a prevalent feeling of pessimism about the long-range results that can be expected to flow from subsidized industrialization. This chapter reflects a felt need to respond to these feelings. The response necessarily involves an analysis of the different types of subsidies employed by the Irish from the standpoint of the efficient use of public funds and the attainment of economic development goals. This is also a chapter of observations and comments stemming from a visit to the Irish scene. Many statements are simply reasoned opinions, thrown out to await possible vindication or refutation as time passes.

PESSIMISM—POTENTIAL ENEMY OF PROSPERITY

The pessimism concerning the future of a subsidized industrialization, and a conscientious concern over the use of tax money in this manner, were voiced by government officials, the man on the street, and businessmen, Irish and foreign. This was not a feeling that in any way overrode support for the two expansion programs. Rather, it was a nagging question in the background— "Is this the right way to be doing it?"—"Some of the firms subsidized have failed, and that's money down the drain."—"Is there too much foreign control of industry coming from these subsidies?" An official connected with the government expressed concern that although only nine firms receiving grants from *An Foras Tionscal* show on the official records as having failed outright, others had gone under and been salvaged in some way. Further questioning the wisdom of grants, he noted that "Most foreign firms turned down for subsidies do not locate here." And at the 1965 stockholders' meeting, the chairman of a well-established Irish firm proudly remarked in his prepared statement:

As you are aware, various inducements of one kind or another have been offered to encourage the development of the country's industrial

activities. It is, therefore, with no little pride that we mention that
the funds for our extensions to date have been provided entirely out
of the company's own resources.[1]

Firms located at the Shannon Industrial Estate come in for more severe
criticism and suspicion than subsidized firms of other locales. A foreign
businessman, himself the recipient of tax exemption subsidies, was sure
firms were only at Shannon for what they could get out of it and would not
stay. An Irish businessman voiced the same sentiments when he noted,
"They're only assembling plants [an erroneous statement]. They've got their
bags packed ready to be off." Another Irish businessman echoed the theme:
"Shannon is a giveaway. Foreign firms will pick up and leave after the tax
remission is gone."

The pessimism in regard to tax-exempt new investment that permeates
the Irishman's thoughts and reflects in his actions is probably a more deep-
seated and potentially dangerous sentiment than the nagging suspicion that
the use of subsidies is in some way unwise or wrong—although the two are
not unconnected. While this lack of optimism for Ireland's industrial future
was somewhat evident in the East around Dublin, where some government
officials would comment on how recent the prosperity was, and how bad things
had been in 1957, its natural breeding ground was the West—around Shannon,
where the newness of the Industrial Estate and the repetition of factory design give an appearance of model blocks from the architect's studio; and in
nearby Ennis, where Gaelic, not English, is overheard when walking along,
and the sleepy indolence of the country town almost denies there's a factory
or two around; and in the once-bustling Spanish trading seaport of Galway,
now dotted with several new factories, at least one of which, rumor has it,
will be shutting down any week now.

It was this pessimism, dominant in the West of Ireland, which a government official intimately associated with the programs, and himself a product
of the western town of Tipperary, referred to when he said he wished there
was a feeling in Ireland such as exists in the United States—a feeling of
optimism, of potential success. And while the success of the First Program
is measured in part by its positive effect upon the spirit of the people, there
is still a sad lack of the buoyancy associated with the type of feeling that
de Toqueville found in Jacksonian America—a feeling of no boundaries being
set to the efforts of man, that man has only to attempt what is not yet done.
There is little of the confidence with which Americans seem gifted and which
gave rise to the saying during World War II: the impossible we do today; the
miraculous will have to wait until tomorrow!

The American-Irish contrast of spirit was exceedingly evident in the
comments of the executives of the two nationalities. Americans were exuber-
ant over the recent expansion of industrial activity in Ireland. One commented,

"In another five years this place will break wide open. I can see the vast change just over the past two years. The Irish are too close to it, they can't see the change." Another, located at Shannon, foresaw the Second Program being exceeded 100 per cent, noting how conservative the First Program's goals had been, and how they had been attained twice over in actuality. He also foresaw the possibilities of vast increases in trade with the European Economic Community, and, rather than feeling Shannon would close down with entry into the European Economic Community, said one day Ireland easily might be doing more business in the export sphere with the European Economic Community than with England.

Among many Irish executives, the world was entirely different. They felt the lowering of tariffs was likely to hurt their firm badly: they could not compete in the rough world of international trade when they did not have funds for research; nor could they withstand the dumping that would take place. Or, if their firm was doing well under the recent spell of prosperity, they recounted tales of the other firms in the neighborhood that were in trouble. Firms that laid off employees in slack periods were interpreted as going out of business, and firms that were not based upon agriculture were catalogued as "artificial"—as opposed to "real" or "permanent."

The pessimism of the executives in the West is undoubtedly a contagious element found in the economic-social milieu of the area, and it afflicts the thoughts of workers, farmers, and townspeople, as well as managers. This section of Ireland, in contrast to Cork or Dublin, has been since time immemorial an agricultural area. The ways and thoughts of an agricultural community have been instilled in each succeeding generation over the centuries. It is the part of Ireland that gives the Emerald Isle its reputation for being a country where time stands still, where the year 700 and its history are strewn on the hillside, seeming to indicate the past demands allegiance, controls the country, and the future. Factories are alien, suspect. They are not part of the established order of things, of Nature. It is a country where the same plot of rocky soil and whitewashed farmhouse have often been in the family for 500 years. It has never been industrialized. Trading villages have flourished for a time. There have been large factories that have lasted many years. But in the end they're gone. The land, the sheep, the customs and thoughts of an agricultural way of life remain, along with the Catholic Church. These are eternal.

It is in this region that industry is a sojourner, an alien suspect as to motive. Factory work is looked down upon. It is said that the nuns advise girls to take lower paid typing jobs rather than do factory work. There is the story of the girls who were card punchers for IBM machines that were located in a factory building. When being told at a dance that they were factory workers, they returned to work the following day ready to quit. Their superior had to convince them they were really office workers, and were just located in a particular type of building that resembled a factory. Many executives spoke of workers whom they knew had taken jobs in England doing factory work when they would not take such jobs at home because of the social stigma attached to the factory worker.[2] Here when an industry folds it is the talk of the pubs for months, and there is a sadistic delight taken in it by the local gentry who always foresaw the event. It is in such an atmosphere that one Shannon executive jokingly suggested all workers be required to wear a sign saying "I believe."

From counties such as these flow the emigrants; and in such astounding numbers that many villages appear desolate, politicians worry about being left without constituents, and a government expansion program has been devised to provide jobs at home to stem this threat to the nation's existence. Not all go to England, from where the home ties are kept alive. It is said that the next parish West after Kerry is America. And one employer complained that it took him six months to train employees who very often quit after one year of work in response to wanderlust desires to see America or Australia.

Both the economic and social situation in the West suggest that further emphasis should be given to creating poles of economic activity, rather than encouraging the scattering of industry over the island through differentiation of subsidy allowances.[3] The Irish are aware of the recent work in location theory[4] and the economic advantages to be achieved from a certain concentration of industry. And although there are political stumbling blocks, differentials in grants for underdeveloped and developed areas as designated in the past have been all but eliminated. After all, all of Ireland is relatively under-industrialized. Hostility toward industry might diminish were it to become a more dominant part of the scenery. More important, one industry's coming or going would not be so noteworthy as to occupy the conversants of the pubs for months. And while nature lovers, or parish priests wishing to preserve the way of life of the parish, may object to industrial centers, Ireland, through the machinery of a democratic government, has endorsed a program of industrialization to raise the living standards of its people and give them an opportunity to earn a living in Ireland. She wants to take her place among modern nations, and this has its costs.

Industry that is locating in Ireland primarily to export is being attracted by subsidies and other advantages such as available labor and market demand or access conditions, to name the more important. This industry must compete in the competitive international field where risks face the firm that do not face it in a domestic market. Moreover, because of the regulation that subsidized industry cannot compete in the Irish market with Irish manufacturers, the stability of a domestic market is denied these firms. Even where such risks as foreign government hostility, tariff changes, quota decreases, or restricted market outlets do not face the exporting firm, its goods are going to be subject to changes in demand conditions. Certainly some products will be discontinued for this latter reason, and it may be that where, for example, a subsidiary of a foreign firm is manufacturing in Ireland items no longer in demand in export markets, it will close down its operations. Relatively swift response to demand conditions is one of the beauties of a market economy; moreover a market economy is characterized by the profit motive and the assumption of risk. This is what gives it its dynamism and its malleability. It deals out rewards for entrepreneurial ability, but its uncertainties also mean there will be some firms that fail, and not all failures could have been avoided even if the firms had had access to the best of managerial talent.

While the above is elementary, it has pertinency for the comments made by the government official who counted each failure with alarm, and in connection with the ideas prevalent in the West of Ireland that there is something suspect about the whole system when its parts, its firms, are not permanent. Actually, over time, the attempt to industrialize can be viewed as a flow of economic activity which must grow larger as a whole, but which must inevitably have deletions as well as additions. Some of the firms will never get off their feet; and some will drop by the wayside as change takes place. By granting subsidies the government has agreed to share the risks of a market economy oriented toward exports; it must expect some failures. "Waste is a part of the price of economic progress; an irrational refusal to pay the price means that nothing will be purchased."[5]

A MACRO OR COST-BENEFIT APPROACH TO SUBSIDY EVALUATION

Implementation tools such as grants and tax exemption should be viewed as a cost of implementing a development program through indirect methods, rather than government ownership, and their health should be judged by taking a look at aggregate new investment induced and the return on total investment, not by isolating individual cases. The returns are not yet in on the government's investment, nor were figures available to inquirers of just what the government's total subsidy costs have been since planning began, as compared to the increased revenue from tax-paying employees and other returns accruing from subsidy-influenced industrial investment.

Foreign firms have brought with them many assets that it would be hard to put a price tag on. Of prime importance for the goal of increasing exports is the access to marketing outlets that small Irish firms lacked. Foreign exchange earnings for a country that must import raw materials and manufactured goods are an important by-product of the new exports. Managerial know-how, probably one of Ireland's pivotal scarcities, is another import of high value. And of course, the influx of foreign capital means that Ireland is able to industrialize without stringent policies to curb consumption and induce savings. As has been noted by many writers, foreign investment permits an earlier development of a country than would otherwise exist, and diminishes the sacrifice of current consumption of the people.

It is true that the use of foreign capital may give rise to future balance of payments problems when repatriation takes place. However, the possibility that periodic balance of payment strains may develop in future years does not of itself warrant a reversal of the policies Ireland is using to achieve industrialization *via* the attraction of foreign private capital to the island. Temporary strains upon the balance of payments during periods of large repatriation or declines in the rate of foreign capital inflow can be handled by influencing, directly or indirectly, various components of the balance of payments. And foreign firms that increase exports will make a direct contribution to foreign exchange earnings and the ability of a country to afford higher standards of living through trade.

Generally, both theoretical and empirical considerations reveal a predominance of advantages over disadvantages flowing from the use of foreign capital by less industrialized countries as a spur to development. In the nineteenth century many of today's industrialized countries were aided in their industrialization by the inflow of foreign funds, and without experiencing insurmountable balance of payments problems. In fact, there is evidence to support the conclusion that the debtor countries often benefited more than the creditor countries from the international flow of capital in the last century. Much of this capital was in the form of private portfolio investment. It is tempting to speculate upon the possibility of Ireland, which up to now has experienced a large amount of direct foreign investment, starting a revival of the nineteenth and early twentieth century popularity of indirect, portfolio investment. Simply by publicizing and promoting opportunities for portfolio investment in the "Old Sod," Ireland could probably attract savings in mass from Australia, America, Canada, and England!

Theoretical reasoning also supports the argument that there are large advantages to be gained from using foreign capital:

> ...it is advantageous for an economy to borrow if its residents can hire funds at a lower cost per unit than the resulting net product is worth. If value added per worker is $100 per year greater when combined with $800 extra capital obtained from abroad at an annual cost of $60, it is to the employer's advantage to borrow this capital. This means that some of the extra domestic product 'belongs' to foreign lenders, but that there is also a surplus for the resident entrepreneur who borrowed these funds. Moreover, there is usually some capital-widening as well as capital-deepening, so these borrowed funds may result in more workers being employed in the modern capitalist sector instead of engaging in traditional subsistence cultivation. It is therefore very much in the interest of all truly underdeveloped countries that international capital be available to them at a low rate, and that individual producers use enough so that its marginal value product equals its unit cost.[6]

Despite the pitfalls in trying to assess and put price tags on costs and benefits,[7] calculated estimates would be beneficial in at least two respects: first, it would be a rough guide to what the government is getting in return for a not inconsiderable outlay of tax-payer's funds, so that should subsidy funds be yielding a low return, alternative implementation tools might be investigated. Secondly, it would propound a macro approach in the justification for the use of subsidies that would alleviate some of the mistrust of the soundness of the implementation tool, and subtract some of the opprobrium attached to the acceptance of subsidies by a firm. This is not to say subsidies should be without suspicion. The micro[8] aspects of types of subsidies and their efficiency will be discussed subsequently in this chapter. But to continue the arguments in favor of a macro approach to accompany the micro approach, there would seem to be sound political and economic benefits to be derived from including the former approach.

Politically the government is always on the carpet to explain and defend a program that is destined to reap vast changes in the whole profile of a country and the way of life of its people. It is not in admiration, but politically to discredit the *Taoiseach* (Prime Minister), that he is called a "gambler." The cost-benefit approach can take the sting out of this name-calling by justifying risk assumption in the light of gains to be reaped, or already evident. Moreover it would put before the public, in black and white figures, as is expected in a country as fervently attached to democratic practices as Ireland, the total amount of money spent in subsidies, the total amount foregone in tax exemption, and the return on this money that has been invested in the industrialization programs of Ireland, and in its future as a country. When such figures are clandestinely undisclosed, this alone causes suspicion to surround them. Aggregate figures would not breach the confidence of any firm, and could serve to create good will towards these firms.

Carefully handled, this approach could have desired educational effects and smooth the economic transition period Ireland is currently undergoing. Those disparaging the Shannon operation because the firms are believed to be likely to leave upon expiration of the subsidies would have to deal with the benefits twenty-five years of operation at Shannon could produce for the economy. Foreign firms would understand more fully than presently why they are receiving subsidies. This could increase their self-esteem and impart a feeling of participation in the programs. Moreover, if it is determined that there are certain temporary drawbacks to doing business in Ireland, and that subsidies are granted to increase the return on investment of firms operating at higher costs because of these drawbacks, publication of such thinking could, simply through educational enlightenment, increase the satisfaction of firms operating as foreign firms on Irish soil. One executive was full of complaints about slow deliveries for local supplies, lack of mechanical skill among workers, poor telephone service, and several other shortcomings of doing business in Ireland. When it was suggested that these were perhaps, in part, growing pains, and that subsidies should compensate him for inconveniences and their extra costs such as those mentioned, he admitted he had not thought of it that way, but realized it made sense.

In addition, an educational return would accrue to the planners themselves in the form of the responsibility to present a reasoned defense of additional pounds spent by the government on subsidies by taking a look at the marginal social productivity of such pounds.[9] And such a presentation could replace the rambling justifications and wandering accusations bestowed upon subsidies by members of the *Dail* (Parliament) during Question Time.

A MICRO APPROACH TO SUBSIDY EVALUATION

The micro approach is not isolated from, but inter-connected with the macro approach, and it rescues the macro approach from becoming a mechanical end-justifies-the-means type of reasoning. The type of subsidy devised, its effect upon the equity of the tax base, and the efficiency with which it is administered, all affect the return on the subsidies invested in the industrialization program; and a look at how much money goes down the drain, as the government official expressed it, is another way of saying that accountability to the public in the use of public funds and responsibility to avoid corruption in the attainment of program goals, no matter how vital and desired these goals may be, should be of concern to any democratic government resting on inherited concepts of justice and right as they have evolved in the Western world.

It is this concern over the means of obtaining ends that often has pitted economists against the use of subsidies.[10] While information crucial to a thorough analysis of the political-economic acceptability of the subsidy program in Ireland—e.g., details concerning the firms that failed, or exactly how recipients are decided upon—was not forthcoming upon request, some judgments can be made based upon the information available and the empirical data of the last chapter. The remaining paragraphs of this chapter will be devoted to comments and conclusions emanating from such sources; but the caveat is repeated that it is not a complete analysis of the use of subsidies to implement goals under the Irish expansion programs.

TAX EXEMPTION

In allowing tax exemption on new exports ranging from 15 to 25 years, Ireland was influenced by the economic necessity, as the planners see it, to increase exports in order to industrialize. The home market could not offer the increase in demand necessary to create enough new investment and new jobs to raise perceptibly the living standards of the populace. This subsidy is open to foreign and domestic exporters. It has developed, so far at least, that foreigners have contributed close to 80 per cent of the new investment, the majority of it in the export field. Irish manufacturers with established firms have not been able to enlarge exports greatly above the levels at which they were exporting in 1955/56. Their old exports are not subject to the 15-25 year subsidies. Moreover, the Irish have not established new firms for exporting nearly as fast as foreign investors have. The existence of this type of subsidy, then, has meant the erosion of equity in the tax base to some extent. Businesses that are not exporters, and older firms whose established exports are not tax exempt, are paying taxes amounting to approximately 47 per cent of profits, whereas new firms, that is, mostly foreign firms, are allowed exemption from taxes for a set period of time.

There is, perhaps, some merit in the argument that Irish firms, through tariff protection, low-cost credit, and in other ways, have been heavily subsidized in the past and have not shown the aggressiveness necessary to achieve industrial development, so that now it is time to see what foreign capital can do—especially in the competitive international trade area where research facilities, patented products, managerial sophistication, and marketing outlets give such firms a high probability of success in exporting. But this type of argument is slipping back over into a macro approach. From a micro standpoint, Ireland's tax subsidy is not equitable, and hence not permanently desirable.

Ireland has provided 100 per cent corporate tax relief for from 10 years (outside Shannon) to 25 years (at Shannon) on new exports. The last year for the 10 years' full relief was to have been 1964. The Second Program, however, recommends extension of this period.[11] Firms not making a profit, of course, do not receive this subsidy, so that tax relief subsidies go to successful firms.

Most foreign firms would have been paying somewhat lower taxes in Ireland than in their home country without the tax exemption. For example, the following listing shows taxes for several countries compared to those in Ireland.

Prior to tax relief, then, Ireland was definitely competitive in regards to tax rates on corporate income. There are several factors that might have influenced her desire to improve her relative tax position further. For example, 100 per cent exemption might have been influenced by transportation costs to markets outside Ireland; by the extra costs the firm might incur by locating in Ireland over the next 10 to 25 years because of a lack of infrastructure and government services; or by the fact that other countries, or areas, such as the Bahamas, Northern Ireland, Puerto Rico, and Southern Italy, also offer subsidies of various sorts to foreign firms. Apparently, however, there was no official economic rationale behind the size of the subsidy. Nor did Parliamentary debate delve into the question of why export tax exemption was to be 100 per cent for 10 to 25 years, depending upon location. There was some attempt to attract foreign firms with an exemption of 50 per cent prior to 1957, and apparently the results were not felt to be large enough, or to come in fast enough. The ante was then raised to 100 per cent.

TABLE 13

BUSINESS TAXES IN SELECTED COUNTRIES

Austria:	51.9 per cent on profits
Belgium:	30 per cent on distributed profits; 25 per cent to 30 per cent cent on undistributed profits
Denmark:	44 per cent corporate income tax
France:	50 per cent corporate income tax; value added tax—25 per cent
Germany:	51 per cent retained earnings tax; 15 per cent distributed earnings tax
Greece:	35 per cent corporate income tax plus 15 per cent surtax = 40.25 per cent
Ireland:	31.67 per cent corporate income tax plus corporation profit tax of 15 per cent = 46.67 per cent
Netherlands:	42 per cent corporate income tax on profits less than $13,000; 57 per cent corporate income tax on profits over $10,000
Spain:	30 per cent corporate income tax; withholding tax on dividends of 8 per cent to 30 per cent
United Kingdom:	38.75 per cent corporate income tax plus profits tax of 15 per cent = 53.75 per cent
United States:	47 per cent corporate income tax on income in excess of $25,000; 25 per cent tax on first $25,000

Source: *The European Markets,* New York: The Chase Manhattan Bank, January, 1964, pp. 55-58.

Theoretically, it is desirable from the aspect of efficiency in the use of public funds for tax exemption to be of such a size as to attract the maximum new investment at the minimum cost. Doubt can be cast upon the need for Ireland to have increased the tax relief to 100 per cent. Of course, practically speaking, at the time this was done no one envisioned subsidies as being a dominant implementation tool and having the results they have had. However, viewed from a micro aspect, it must be said that tax exemption as a type of subsidy is open to the criticisms that it is hard to tell in advance what size exemption is required to achieve a given goal, it is time-consuming to experiment with increasing the subsidy in small steps to avoid over-subsidizing, and the size of the subsidy may be out of the country's independent determination where there is international competition to attract foreign capital by tax relief. In connection with this last point, the varieties of subsidies can vary so as to confuse comparisons among countries. One tax analyst has concluded, however, that "Ireland offers as much, if not more, in the way of tax incentives than any other country in the world. Yes, even more than Puerto Rico." [12]

Bearing in mind the unplanned nature of the subsidy's size, it is interesting to look at evidence of the efficiency of tax exemption on export profits as attested to by the sample. Among the 26 firms that exported 30 per cent or more of their sales, 19 listed government subsidies as "very important." Thirty-five per cent of these 26 firms said they would not have invested without government subsidies, that is, 9 of the 26 firms; 10 gave inconclusive answers; 1 gave no answer. Twenty-two per cent, or 6 firms, said they would have invested without the tax exemption. The inconclusive answers leaned toward a negative response to the question of whether they would have invested without subsidies, more than toward a positive reply. It will be recalled that this group of 10 firms giving inconclusive answers made a major contribution to the economy, and was characterized by a predominance of firms that listed more than two factors as playing a major role in the investment decision—most often labor, market, and government subsidies.

Considering that most, if not all, of the 19 firms giving "no" or inconclusive answers had higher taxes in their home countries than in Ireland, we may ask whether a good number of these firms would have invested with a lower subsidy in the form of a fewer number of years of tax exemption or a lower exemption rate, or a combination of both? There are at least a couple of hypotheses that can be set up in considering this question. First, if factors other than subsidies played a large enough part in the investment decision to make it possible investment would have taken place without *any* subsidy—and there were more than one of these additional factors in a good number of cases—then it is plausible that a lower subsidy would have done the trick for a number of the 10 inconclusive firms. Five of these 10 firms, however, gave evidence of being able to locate in other areas of the world where subsidies are given and labor is available.

A second hypothesis concerning the firms which gave "no" answers can be derived from the fact that these firms showed the highest percentage listing of government grants along with tax exemption and thus admitted a high dependence upon subsidies. For this group, lower subsidies in the tax exemption field (which is tied to profits) might have been acceptable as long as capital needs in the form of grants were forthcoming.

The above hypotheses are inclusive, however, and they concern a group that has contributed more to the economy than the group that would have invested without any subsidy. In fact, the sample gives more evidence to support the following statement: in the example of tax exemption it appears the *Taoiseach* (Prime Minister) has bid his hand well. After all, there were only 6 cases out of 26 heavily committed to exporting where Ireland could have definitely attracted the new business units without subsidies.

Looking at the subsidy-influenced increase in exports further, there is evidence from the sample that new firms are helping to diversify Ireland's export market. Many new firms are finding Ireland a good point of distribution to several markets, thus weakening Ireland's dependence upon the United Kingdom market. However, there does not appear to be a tendency for another dominant industrial export market to develop comparable to the United Kingdom market (even considering European Economic Community countries as one market). Nor was there any evidence that export tax relief encouraged a foreign firm to seek additional foreign markets; rather, firms locating in Ireland seemed to have marketing outlets already established.

Shannon is contributing to this diversification with its business units that ship by air to world markets. And the Shannon operations as a group seemed to have at least two important evidences of permanency: First, there was a looking forward to European Economic Community membership by a majority of the firms, and a feeling that any real threats to Shannon by Ireland's entry would be negotiable. After all, Shannon is located in an under-industrialized area of a relatively unindustrialized country, and the European Economic Community provides accommodations for schemes by its members designed to develop such areas. Secondly, firms had already been located in Shannon long enough, and Shannon itself was growing rapidly enough, that members of the Estate had developed vested interests in its continued prosperity, and felt its growth into an industrial enclave would benefit their operations. Thus, Shannon should now have internal forces other than the Irish governmental agency working for its future.

There is reason to believe subsidies are higher than necessary at Shannon. While all firms mentioned subsidies as being important or very important, 3 of the 9 would have invested without subsidies, and 4 out of the 9 gave inconclusive answers. Only 2 of the firms listed grants as important; 5 listed labor. It seems implausible to suggest that the Shannon area has now, or will have in the next 25 years, enough drawbacks over other areas of Ireland to warrant the subsidy differential, especially since many of the firms there are obtaining advantageous cost conditions from the use of relatively cheap labor available in the area.

The lack of influence of grants at Shannon upon the investment decision seems to result from the fact that many of the firms were subsidiaries of large foreign firms which could provide any initial capital needed to set up operations. Thus, in the total investment picture the grants were relatively small compared to tax exemption, and of negligible importance. Where grants were important there was evidence of the firms being on shaky financial ground, and possibly in one case, not giving the government a good return on funds invested.

By using export tax exemption to attract foreign firms, but then limiting the sales of these firms to the export market (with the exception of a token amount of domestic sales in some cases) the Irish government may have painted itself into a political corner. Since Ireland is subsidizing these exporting firms, it is felt it would be unfair to allow competition on the domestic market; moreover such competition would intensify resentment against foreign capitalists. At the same time, Ireland is following a policy of tariff lowering and expects to enter the European Economic Community. This will, once the tariffs are low enough or the membership in the European Economic Community attained, allow imports into Ireland of many of the goods produced by foreign firms located in Ireland and exporting the same goods from Ireland. At least two of the latter type of firms interviewed mentioned an intention to press the Irish government for increased Irish market sales because of this eventuality. One businessman expressed the belief that foreign firms with a stake in the domestic market of Ireland would be less likely to leave upon expiration of the effect of subsidies. This would seem to make economic sense, and is supported by the fact that the sample showed the larger the firm's domestic market, the less strategic were subsidies in the investment decision. Moreover, foreign export firms limited to the export market may not be contributing the highest value of which they are capable to the industrialization of Ireland. As Dr. W. J. L. Ryan, head of Ireland's planning, points out,

> ...present inducements appear to have been successful in expanding existing exports and in establishing new export industries. If there is danger in these developments, it lies in the possibility of many of the new export industries being 'export-import enclaves'—that is, industries which import the bulk of their materials and export almost all their output. Such industries might have no direct impact on existing activities—these latter would only benefit indirectly through the expenditure of the new incomes of the workers in the new industries. The new export industries might not be meshed into the existing industrial structure—there might be no 'backward linkages,' and there might, therefore, be no strong pressures, emanating from the new activities, on existing industries to improve their methods and techniques. Moreover, the new export industries might exert little pressure towards the creation of industries at earlier stages of production. [13]

But the fact remains that these foreign firms on Irish soil are subsidized more heavily than domestic firms in most cases since domestic producers are not allowed tax exemption except on increased exports, and many produce only for home market consumption. Having bolstered such firms with the adaptation grants in order to allow the efficient to survive the lowering of tariffs, it is hardly politically possible to inundate them with competition from more heavily subsidized foreign firms on the island. As Americans have found in such examples as that of cotton, subsidies tend to proliferate, become complicated, and terribly messy. Moreover, they are often more disruptive of political consensus than economic conditions created by the "impersonal" forces of the market.

GRANTS

In examining government equipment and machinery grants in Ireland, the size of these grants is explained by such considerations as a desire by *An Foras Tionscal* (The Grant Board) to see that enough of the investing firm's money is in the business to place a burden of risk upon the investors and give them a stake in the firm's future success. The size of grant has also been used to influence investment location. There was no explanation to be found in documents, or coaxed from government officials, as to why grants are considered necessary to go along *with* tax exemption to attract new investment after the decision to quit favoring certain locations with under-developed area differentials. As originally designed, the underdeveloped area grants were not seen as a large-scale implementation tool within the larger context of a development program designed to attract foreign capital. Foreign firms seem to have benefited from grants because of extension of the original program aimed at the areas of heavy emigration, rather than any closely reasoned approach to the economic rationale behind this type of subsidy, or the total size of subsidy needed to do the job, tax exemption in-cluded.

As a subsidy type, some economists prefer the equipment or factory grant above tax exemption.[14] It is usually designed so that it is a smaller subsidy than tax exemption, and rather than going to the profitable, it is seen as helping firms with the initial expenses involved in getting on their feet. The idea is that such expenses can thwart investment entirely, or exhaust the financial resources, of a potentially successful firm. Had such ideas circu-lated behind the walls of *An Foras Tionscal,* there probably would not have been the complaint by the small Irish businessman, whose application for a grant was pending and highly uncertain, that he had reservations about the expansion program because the government planned for larger type factories, and the smaller types were not envisioned in their scheme.

The impressions left by executive interviews, as well as the data given in the preceding chapter showing 21 new firms of the sample listing tax exemption as important, compared to 11 listing grants as important, give reasons to doubt grants are a necessary complement to tax exemption in the attraction of new firms to Ireland. Yet, as far as can be discerned from inter-views with government officials, including officials of *An Foras Tionscal,* grants are administered as though firms were very likely not to invest without grants, and hence as though grants were carrying the heavy burden of deciding what type of new firm will be most beneficial to the economy.

An Foras Tionscal says it does not have a formula in deciding upon recipients, which is probably true in the narrow sense; but it *does* decide how to allot funds, and seems to have reasons for its decisions. These reasons are criteria derived from the over-all expansion program goals, such as a need to increase exports and employment, and a desire to industrialize the country; and they are applied apparently in a way so that priority is given to those business operations that seem most *surely* destined to fulfill such goals. The result has been that foreign firms setting up relatively large operations measured in terms of pounds invested in plant and equipment have been the largest recipients—not on the basis of need, but on the basis of not needing! Such criteria make this type of subsidy of questionable political and economic value in the Irish situation.

As currently operating in the Irish economy this subsidy has brought cries of discrimination from the domestic firms with small operations and less chances of success, especially in exporting, than well-established foreign firms, which are viewed as contributing more to program goals and hence considered more worthy of subsidization. Should this situation be changed in an attempt to exclude firms not needing assistance and likely to invest without grants, undoubtedly such firms, investing large amounts and contributing immediately to balance of payment improvement for Ireland, would feel discriminated against. This "frying-pan-into-the-fire" result might be avoided by cutting the subsidy down considerably in scope so that firms not receiving them do not feel themselves to be a minority. Such a possibility is considered below; but it is evident that it is hard to design the group receiving this type of subsidy so that it is considered by all to be an equit-able subsidy. As it is now designed and operating in Ireland, grants appear to be going to a good many firms that would have invested without them. It may be, of course, that *An Foras Tionscal* can open its files to evidence to the contrary.

GRANTS VERSUS TAX EXEMPTION

Since equipment and machinery grants have been dispensed in Ireland as though they were a major drawing card for new firms, especially foreign ones, it is interesting to compare this type of subsidy with the tax exemption subsidy as though they were separate, alternative implementation tools, and see which ranks higher in efficiency.

To begin with, grants definitely have higher administrative expenses because their size must be determined by a detailed examination of the firm, and because the group is not so well designed that this type of subsidy is automatically allowed to all applicants, as is tax exemption on exports. There is more opportunity for government corruption or patronage in the use of grants than with tax exemption. While such corruption may not exist in actuality, the administration of a grant program where there is governmental discretion, as the one in Ireland, creates an aura of suspicion and invites political attack.

Tax exemption subsidizes those who have proven they can operate profit-ably in the Irish environment, and as set up in Ireland, requires that a firm must stay in business 15 years or more to receive the full subsidy. Grants for machinery, equipment, and working capital are dispensed at the beginning of operations; if the firm fails, the government stands to lose the entire subsidy. Thus, while tax exemption is the larger subsidy as both subsidies are currently operated in Ireland, the return on investment is undoubtedly higher for tax exemption on exports.

To cut the scope of the grant might help the return, and would be a salving political prescription. If the government wants to share risk with private enterprises of certain types, size, etc., that might have trouble getting started without government aid in order to increase industrial activity and provide some of the growth perspective that is lacking in the private economy's outlook, it would very likely depend upon grants to do this, as it has in the case of adaptation grants. But in the Irish example, such grants could be considered less a major tool in terms of achieving initial aggregate economic contributions to the expansion program goals, and more of a supplementary subsidy—a subsidy whose major contribution might very well show up in the longer run by an increase in entrepreneural spirit and talent among the Irish.

If such a change were inaugurated, Irish firms would stand as much of a chance of obtaining such subsidies as foreign firms of a comparable nature. In other words, the group receiving the subsidy would be redefined so as to favor Irish firms more than they are now favored, and at the same time, cut down the size of the total grants in aggregate. Total administration expenses might very well rise, and *An Foras Tionscal* would have to think through carefully the formula to be used in dispensing such grants in order to improve their political respectability over their current reputation. The Shannon Industrial Estate might eliminate such grants, depending upon the type of firm it wished to attract to the Estate.

There is, of course, the problem that Northern Ireland gives a plant and equipment subsidy of up to 33 1/3 per cent of the cost of such expenditures, and the Republic of Ireland is definitely in competition with this area. However, it will be remembered the sample showed that, of those firms shipping 10-15 per cent of their sales to the United Kingdom, most said they would have invested without government subsidies; and of the 6 new firms investing because of the United Kingdom market, and shipping more than 15 per cent to that market, 5 said they were unable to say whether or not government subsidies were necessary to encourage their investment. Rather, it would appear that these firms were highly influenced by labor as well as market and government subsidies. Thus, the Republic of Ireland has the advantage of tax exemption which Northern Ireland cannot offer, and more attractive labor conditions to offset the bids of Northern Ireland. [15]

INDUSTRIAL CREDIT

Industrial Credit Company aid to companies in need of funds to get started or enlarge might be considered as an *alternative* to the use of grants. Suggestion for this stems from the comments of an Irish executive. His firm was in line for an adaptation grant, and he had just listed such grant "of little importance" on the interview scale, while listing Industrial Credit Company funds as "very important." He said: "It is the availability of money that is far more important than a grant *per se*. It's the money that holds you back."

If the Industrial Credit Company should operate according to the precepts of an industrial development bank, ready to take an active role in encouraging new investment and sharing risks with firms that could not get started alone, in the form of loans, common or preferred stock, then the disposal of funds as carried out by *An Foras Tionscal* might be discontinued. Moreover, there would be enough funds available to the Industrial Credit Company to continue its operations of offering loans to "well-heeled" businesses wanting to borrow money and contributing heavily to program goals, as well as small operations covered under the suggested new approach. Subsidies would most likely be needed to encourage investment on the scale desired, and they could take the form of low interest rates and lenient terms for repayment. Such a form of subsidy would seem to be more acceptable in regard to size and type than grants. In addition, they could be more easily designed than grants for the needs of the business receiving it without cries of discrimination.

At the present time loans from the Industrial Credit Company are given as supplements to grants in many cases. But should grants be dispensed with, and loans used to encourage investment where it would not take place without governmental aid, there is reason to believe the Industrial Credit Company would show even more hesitancy than *An Foras Tionscal* to play the role of a daring or imaginative assumer of risks promising only longer run benefits. The success of such a change would hinge upon the ability of the people administering it to remove the conservative dark suit of a traditional banker and don the plaid sportcoat of an aggressive industrializer, and be willing to lose a few shirts in the process.

SUMMARY

The preceding paragraphs of comments, suggestions, commendations, and critical appraisal constitute only a partial analysis of the use of subsidies in the Irish expansion programs as a major tool for the implementation of program goals. Major gaps in information preclude a full analysis. A summary of the thinking of this chapter in capsule form can tie together the main elements.

There is a need to clarify and defend the reasons the government is using subsidies on a large scale to help Ireland achieve industrialization at the pace envisioned by the two expansion programs. Such a need stems from several facts:

1. Much of Ireland is an agriculturally based society that has never become accustomed to the pattern of living and thinking that an industrialized community imposes upon its people, for better or worse, and industrial subsidization is received in many parts of Ireland not as a panacea, but with suspicion that it is siphoning off aid which might be going to agriculture, and with pessimism that, besides diverting government policy from emphasis and concern for agriculture, industrialization will waste such funds completely, because factories are not "real," that is, not lasting or indigenous to Ireland. The workers are not alone in this feeling; it permeates echelons of high responsibility.

2. Government officials do not exhibit unanimous conviction that by dispensing subsidies the government is doing the "right" thing. They have been uneasy about losses and charges of corruption, and they have not derived formulas for dispensing such aid in which they have enough confidence to defend publicly.

3. Many firms receiving the subsidies are not sure what they are given for, if anything, and executives exhibit pricks of conscience from the popular feeling that subsidy-influenced investment is tainted or inefficient.

4. Many firms not receiving subsidies resent them since the majority of the subsidy money has gone to foreigners and relatively large firms. There is the likelihood such resentment will grow if the lowering of tariffs and entry into the European Economic Community bring about competition in the Irish market from subsidized foreign firms.

It was suggested that both empirical data and theoretical economic arguments could be helpful in clarifying the rationale behind the use of subsidies in the Irish situation, and evaluating their performance. Theoretically, there would seem to be a need to view Ireland's attempt to industrialize by indirect manipulation of private enterprise from the perspective of the economy as a whole, that is, from a macro perspective. The macro approach would involve, among other things:

1. The establishment of a review system of the effects of subsidies upon the economy in the light of program goals. This would involve cost-benefit studies looking into the total costs to the economy as a whole and the returns accruing to the economy from subsidized investment. It would mean looking at additional returns that continuation

of the subsidy program would reap for the economy, that is, the marginal social productivity of tax money so spent, in comparison to alternative expenditures of such money. It could serve to enlighten both the planners and the public. While such studies would involve many estimates and could only be used as rough guides, a reasoned approach should be the background upon which strategy is developed, and should have more than educational value.

2. The viewing of failures of subsidized firms and shut-downs as inevitable where the rules of the market economy call the tune and the government is participating in the game with the calculated intention of using a private economy, indirectly influenced, to help achieve its industrialization targets, rather than suspending the rules and controlling the market to a larger degree. This involves thinking of the program as aiming to increase the flow of industrial activity over time, and expecting there will be changes in the composition of that activity as demand conditions warrant, and as inevitable mistakes are made in assuming the risks of the market-place.

3. Emphasis upon the ends. It is important that a democratic society decide how important the ends are, and then look at alternative ways of achieving those ends; or, where the means involved to achieve fully the desired goals are not acceptable, then it may be necessary to sacrifice complete fulfillment. It is at this point that the ends cannot justify the means. But it is also at this point that it is highly important that the decision to sacrifice complete goal attainment be made in the light of a thorough analysis of the macro type where returns and costs of the subsidy are reviewed. In a democratic regime, such a review can help set the tolerance level for deviations from standards of fiscal responsibility and equity involved in the use of subsidies that the real world may demand of a country trying to industrialize in a hurry.

Empirical evidence outlined in the last chapter gives strong support to the conclusions that subsidies are a dominant causal factor in the rise of new investment in Ireland, and that without subsidies, other things remaining the same, Ireland could not have come close to filling her First Program goals or maintaining the momentum she has under the Second Program for Economic Expansion. Moreover, such new investment has increased foreign exchange earnings, helped to diversify Ireland's exports and their markets, and may very well have given Ireland a more "permanent" group of new industries than she would have had without subsidies. Evidence for the latter statement comes from the fact that the 11 firms that would have invested without subsidies invested less per firm and employed more labor per firm than the group that were more highly influenced by subsidies. If it is true that the higher the investment by a firm the less transient the firm, and that the more labor intensive the firm, the more flexible its location, then investment that was highly influenced by subsidies would appear to be less transient than investment that would have taken place without subsidies.

Besides the need for a macro approach to development goals, there is the need at all times to consider the methods of achieving these goals; and where subsidies are a means, this involves looking at the individual types of subsidies as they are related to fiscal responsibility, accountability, and equity, ends in themselves in the attainment of efficient, just government policies.

There was found to be evidence that tax exemption on export profits is the major attraction to new investors and is making the largest contribution to program goals of increasing industrial investment, exports, and employment. For this reason tax exemption and grants were reviewed separately from a micro standpoint and then compared as alternative instruments for implementing plan goals. The results were as follows: tax exemption as it is designed in Ireland distorts the equity of the tax base, and has created political resentment of a subsidy which in operation has been received by foreigners more than by the Irish. Also, it is hard to be sure Ireland has not allowed a larger exemption than necessary—particularly at Shannon. Weighed in the balance, however, it would appear that tax exemption may very well be a small price to pay for attracting new investment on the scale it has over the past six years, and securing for Ireland investment that might have gone elsewhere had there been no subsidy.

In comparing tax exemption with grants, it is found both distort the tax base and create political accusations of discrimination. Grants are probably more of a focus point of such criticism than tax exemption because of the administrative discretion exercised in their dispersal.

Tax exemption on profits in Ireland goes to the successful. Grants in Ireland have gone to the successful as well as those firms needing help in the early years of establishing a business or in modernizing their business in order to survive. Subsidies should be given to successful firms only when their contributions, singly or in aggregate, are of crucial importance to the economy, and only then if the firms would not invest without them. While data indicate tax exemption to the successful in Ireland may be justified on the basis of the above criteria, there is reason to doubt that grants are needed on so large a scale in combination with tax exemption to attract new investment.

Consideration was given to the advantages of cutting down the number of firms receiving grants, offering them only to those firms needing help in order to start a new firm or expand an old one. Changing the recipients and philosophy in the administration of grants would assuage accusations that grants benefit only foreigners. It should also increase the efficiency of the over-all subsidy program of grants and tax exemption, even though it might mean higher administrative expenses in the dispensation of grants.

Even further efficiency might result from the substitution of loans for grants, and/or government investment in share-capital not for immediate resale.

Notes

1. *The Economist,* (August 14, 1965), 649.

2. It should be noted that for most comparable jobs in England wages and fringe benefits, such as unemployment pay and health insurance benefits, are larger than in Ireland.

3. The United Nations is sending a team of experts to Ireland to advise on research projects in regional planning with special emphasis on the economic aspects of the location of industry.

4. See, for example, Walter Isard and Eugene W. Schooler, "Industrial Complex Analysis, Agglomerate Economies, and Regional Development," *Journal of Regional Science,* I (Spring, 1959), 19-33.

5. A. E. Kahn, "Investment Criteria in Development Programs," *Quarterly Journal of Economics,* LXV (February, 1951), 61.

6. Stephen Enke, *Economics for Development,* Englewood Cliffs, New Jersey: Prentice-Hall, Inc., 1963, p. 451.

7. For an account of estimating accounting prices for Pakistan and using them operationally, see G. F. Papanek and M. A. Quresh, "The Use of Accounting Prices in Planning," in *Organization, Planning and Programming for Economic Development,* Washington: U. S. Government Printing Office, 1964, pp. 95-100. Stephen Enke points out the dangers of chicanery in estimates of this type, and suggests that a good rule to follow in estimating external economies and diseconomies is to include only those about which there is general agreement. See Enke, *op. cit.,* pp. 277-297.

8. "Micro" is used to designate the appraisal of the desirability of using subsidies as an implementation tool in relation to ends other than those of the program, e.g., equity of the tax base; "macro" is used in referring to the aggregate approach where subsidies are considered in the light of how much they contribute to program goals for which they are designed.

9. For literature concerning marginal social productivity theory so prominent in development literature, and its siamese twin, cost-benefit reasoning, see A. E. Kahn, "Investment Criteria in Development," *Quarterly Journal of Economics,* LV (February, 1951), 38-61; H. B. Chenery, "The Application of Investment Criteria," *Quarterly Journal of Economics,* LVII (February, 1953), 76-96; A. O. Hirschman, *The Strategy of Economic Development,* New Haven, Connecticut: Yale University Press, 1960, 76-97; R. N. McKean, "Cost-Benefit Analysis and British Défense Expenditure," *Public Expenditure Appraisal and Control,* Peacock and Robertson (eds.), London: Oliver and Boyd, 1963, pp. 17-35; J. V. Krutilla and Otto Eckstein, *Multiple Purpose River Development,* Baltimore: John Hopkins Press, 1958;

Otto Eckstein, *Water Resource Development,* Boston: Harvard University Press, 1958; J. C. DeHaven, Jack Hirshleifer, and J. W. Milliman, *Water Supply, Economic Technology and Policy,* Chicago: University of Chicago Press, 1960; H. B. Chenery, "Comparative Advantage and Development Policy," *American Economic Review,* LI (March, 1961), 158-186

10. In the United States the closest parallel to subsidies of the Irish type would be subsidies given by the individual communities such as remission of local taxes on industry for a number of years and the building of factories for lease or rent-free occupancy by new firms in a given locale. Studies have shown such subsidies are of a small scale and therefore have not been a major determinant of location of industry. (See, for example, Stefan H. Robock, "Industrialization and Economic Progress in the Southeast," *Southern Economic Journal,* XX (April, 1954), 307-327; G. E. McLaughlin and Stefan H. Robock, *Why Industry Moves South,* National Planning Association, 1949. pp. 107-117; and Victor Roterus, "Community Industrial Development—A Nationwide Survey," U. S. Congress, Senate Committee on Banking and Currency, *Development Corporations and Authorities,* 86th Congress, 1st Session, December, 1959, pp. 123-129.) Criticism has tended to center around the argument that the competing of communities within a given possible location area for a firm results in no net gain for the area, while denying needed sources of revenues for poor communities with limited tax bases, and also around the evidence pointing to the fact that some firms attracted by tax subsidies are "fly-by-night" operations. For arguments pro and con in respect to the use of local tax subsidies by communities in the United States see: John E. Moes, *Local Subsidies for Industry,* Chapel Hill, North Carolina: University of North Carolina Press, 1962, John E. Moes, "Subsidization of Industry by Local Communities in the South," *Southern Economic Journal,* XXXVII (October, 1961), 187-193, and I. J. Goffman and J. H. Thompson, "Replies and Rejoinder," *Southern Economic Journal,* XXIX (October, 1962), 111-126.

11. *Second Program for Economic Expansion,* Part II, Dublin: Stationery Office, 1964, p. 264.

12. Leon O. Stock, "Operation 'Eire Lift'," *Taxes—The Tax Magazine,* XLI (November, 1963), 663.

13. W. J. L. Ryan, *Investment Criteria in Ireland,* a paper read before the Society on November 17, 1961, Dublin: Cahill and Company, Limited

14. See, for example, Benjamin Higgins, *Economic Development,* New York: W. W. Norton and Company, Inc., 1959, p. 515, and M. C. Taylor, *Industrial Tax-Exemption in Puerto Rico,* Madison, Wisconsin: University of Wisconsin Press, 1957, p. 153 and p. 117.

15. To the extent that attractive labor conditions are composed of low-paid female labor, entry into the European Economic Community might lessen Ireland's competitive position inasmuch as in 1964 the European Economic Community ended pay discrimination in all of the six member countries, and for the first time in history women have the same labor rights as male workers.

CHAPTER **8** SUMMARY AND
CONCLUSIONS

PLANNING IN A DEMOCRATIC NATION

In 1958 Ireland instituted economic planning designed to increase low levels of income, reduce high rates of unemployment, and counteract the forces contributing to mass emigration in a stagnant economy highly dependent upon agriculture. Changes involved in the metamorphosis of a predominantly agricultural economy into an economy characterized by a high level of industrial output are not easily wrought. The study of the implementation of industrialization goals under Ireland's First Program for economic expansion provides an account of the manner in which this nascent industrial country achieved initial success in effecting relatively rapid industrial expansion.

Economic planning outlines goals and conceives ways in which these goals may be achieved. Assurance of at least partial achievement of plan objectives generally leads to the need for certain government controls and incentives to influence variables strategic to plan success. This study examines the importance of government control and influence of new investment in the implementation of plan goals for industrialization outlined in the First and Second programs for economic expansion of the Republic of Ireland. The period covered is from 1958 to mid 1964. The study traces the roles played by the major tools of implementation selected by the Irish planners to effect plan goals of industrialization, particularly the strategic goal of increased industrial exports. The tools chosen, and the extent to which each tool was used, involved the necessary dovetailing of implementation devices with democratic institutions, and with a democratic consensus of decided preference for adherence to the general framework of a market economy.

The Irish chose a light network of planning of the type presently used in France. This design of planning emphasizes concerted action by the public and private sectors working in tandem to set plan goals. To the extent that action is inherent in agreement over plan targets, the need for unilateral government concern with implementation is lessened. Voluntary action by a relatively small and unenterprising private sector, however, could not assure the measure of success needed to make headway in solving Ireland's urgent economic problems. The government played a leading role in providing a growth perspective and instituting policies designed to induce a pace of new industrial investment sufficient to promise success in the transition from a predominantly agricultural economy with a small, protected industrial sector, to a developing economy with a competitive industrial sphere.

Ireland's experience with the French type of planning involving dependence upon indirect tools for manipulating the economy to achieve plan goals has not been a problem-proof blueprint for economic expansion. Rather, the importance of Ireland's experience lies with its relative success within the framework of an evolutionary approach to change through the selection of implementation devices that have worked through the existing market economy, and have proven compatible with established democratic procedures.

PLANNING STRATEGY AND RESULTS

The government of Ireland dramatized the possible consequences of the threatened entry of Britain into the European Economic Community, and the high rate of emigration, in order to marshall for action the latent forces of growth in a dormant economy and drifting nation. From 1950 to 1957 Ireland's real gross national product showed no perceptible expansion. Her predominantly agricultural economy was unable to provide jobs for the labor force because of dependence upon agricultural exports that are subject to constricting forces upon demand and prices, and declining manpower needs with mechanization. Her domestic industry was not competitive in international markets, and had ceased to expand once the protected home market was saturated. An assessment of the economy and its potential exposed a lack of managerial talent, raw materials, an expanding domestic market, technological advantages, and foreign marketing channels. Faced with the need to industrialize her economy in order to stem the tide of emigrants and raise the level of income of her population, Ireland adopted policies designed to attract foreign firms with advantages she lacked for international trade, and induce her domestic industries to modernize in order to become competitive.

To accomplish this latter feat, the government lowered tariff barriers and let the fresh winds of international trade fan the fires of competition that long had been quelched by tariff barriers. At the same time the government provided aid in the forms of grants and credit for firms forced to modernize in order to survive under the new conditions. While this may appear drastic action for a democratically responsive government to take, political feasibility was insured by Britain's application for membership in the European Economic Community. If Britain went into the Community without Ireland, the special trade relations currently in effect whereby Ireland has duty-free access to the United Kingdom market could not be maintained. Britain would have to raise the common external tariff wall agreed to by members of the Community. If Ireland entered the European Economic Community, her tariff-sheltered industries would have to give up their protection as a condition of membership in the Common Market, which is working for the abolition of trading barriers among all members. Ireland's future prospects appeared better if she reduced tariffs, improved her competitive position by modernizing her domestic industries, and prepared to enter the European Economic Community if and when Britain entered.

The measures aimed at improving the domestic industrial sector were not enough by themselves to create a pace of industrialization needed to realize growth targets and provide employment opportunities sufficient to lower the emigration rate. To achieve a more rapid industrialization than could be prodded from internal resources alone, Ireland used grants and tax exemption to attract foreign investors which would locate on Irish shores and produce goods for export. By granting 100 per cent tax relief for 10 years on profits from new exports Ireland was able to attract many new firms that would not have located there otherwise. During the five-year period of the First Program, 133 new firms with foreign participation invested in Ireland. Aided by this spur to growth, and propitious external conditions during the period of the First Program, Ireland realized an increase in real gross national product of just over 4 per cent per annum, and a growth rate in the industrial sector of 7 per cent.

Not all the glory belongs to the private sector, however. The First Program was a design for changing the emphasis of public investment from non-industrial areas such as housing to areas such as electricity and fertilizer production. Ireland has a relatively small private sector, and roughly one-third of new industrial investment over the past six years was direct public investment. For the economy as a whole, almost one-half of new fixed capital formation was accounted for by the public sector.

The channeling of public investment into areas designated by a coordinated expansion program contributed to the success of planning in Ireland. But perhaps the greatest contribution of the government was simply providing leadership in the planning efforts and a growth perspective, thus convincing a nation dejected and discouraged by years of turmoil and stagnation that improvement was possible. By "creating a big fuss" the government has started to erode the ingrained strains of pessimism that have lingered since the days of the potato famine.

TOOLS OF IMPLEMENTATION

The study has supported the argument that a necessary adjunct of the success achieved to date by the Irish economy in attaining plan goals of industrialization—goals that involve a heavy commitment of new investment to the industrial export sector—was the government's influence and control of new investment through tax exemption, non-repayable government grants, government credit, and government enterprise. Dominant among these tools of implementation were tax exemption and public investment. Approximately three-fourths of all new fixed capital formation was materially influenced by the aforementioned tools of implementation.

The majority of new private industrial investment was foreign investment attracted by the tax exempt status of profits on exports for 10 years (with a five-year tapering-off period) in areas other than Shannon and for 25 years for firms located at the Shannon Industrial Estate. A survey of 34 firms investing in new plant and equipment between 1958 and July of 1964 showed that government subsidies, markets, and available labor were the dominant causal factors influencing new private investment over the past six years in Ireland, in that order.

Most firms listed more than one factor as an important determinant of investment. However, only 34 per cent of the firms in the sample specifically stated that they would have invested without government subsidies. The remaining 66 per cent either specifically stated that they would not have invested in the absence of government subsidies, or were uncertain. The uncertain replies, ten in all, gave strong reasons to doubt that investment would have taken place in the absence of any subsidies. Moreover, this group of firms, representing 66 per cent of the number of firms interviewed, invested an average of £ 440,000 per firm, £ 200,000 more per firm than firms that stated categorically they would have invested without government subsidies, and provided 741 more jobs for the economy.

The results of the firm interviews lead to the conclusion that without government subsidies industrial investment, exports, and employment would have been well below levels achieved over the past six years, and as a result, the Irish economy would have lacked the momentum needed to create conditions conducive to continued economic expansion.

The particular mix of implementation tools grew out of Ireland's economic heritage, as well as the success (anticipated or not) of the individual tools over the period of planning to date. They were selected for their compatibility with "democratic" planning, and at the same time helped to determine the type of planning that emerged.

Government enterprise had the advantage of providing a direct and accessible route to manipulating the economy by the use of established institutions. The First Program was primarily a design for emphasizing productive investment by the public sector, expanding activities of existing state bodies where necessary. Ireland has approached the establishment of state enterprise from a pragmatic perspective, rather than any dogmatic adherence to ideology, so long as the extent of this type of enterprise is compatible with the continued expansion of a decentralized market economy. Thus, the use of public enterprise as an implementation tool provided an acceptable means for a country with superior talent concentrated in the public service to capitalize upon its limited human resources.

The use of grants and tax exemption, as well as government credit, to achieve economic ends had historical precedent in the Irish economy. These tools were turned to when it was decided to adopt the type of decentralized planning that relies upon the private sector to carry a large share of the responsibility for economic growth. There was, apparently, no preplanned design in regard to the composition or relative roles to be played by public investment, tax exemption, government credit, and government grants. Rather, they were thrown into the hopper, along with other government policies designed to stir action in a stagnant economy. Their use was facilitated by the fact that Ireland, contrary to most countries trying to effect transition from a largely agricultural to an industrial country, has not suffered from an extreme shortage of investment capital.

EVALUATION OF THE MAJOR IMPLEMENTATION TOOLS

A complete evaluation of each of the implementation tools used in the Irish situation would make several studies the size of this one. Certain aspects of the use of government subsidies, government credit, and government enterprise have been isolated, however, in an attempt to compare and analyze these three tools, both in a general way, and as they have been used specifically in the social, political, and economic environment of Ireland.

Public Enterprise

Generally speaking, government enterprise uses a large amount of government funds to achieve a given level of industrial expansion, as compared to government subsidies and government credit. Moreover, experience in many countries has shown government enterprise often exhibits shortcomings in the area of marketing. Ireland's public enterprises, according to observers on the scene, have shown a pattern of weakness in marketing organization, and this has meant that they have not operated as a formidable force in opening up foreign marketing channels—a difficult task, but a vital one for the achievement of plan goals of increased industrial exports.

Looking specifically at the role of public enterprise in the Irish development efforts, the future expansion of government investment as a dynamic component of the Irish economy is limited in at least two respects. First, because of Ireland's political-economic attachment to a predominantly decentralized market economy, government enterprise is acceptable only with limits, and these limits may be approached within the early years of the Second Program if the Program itself is a guide. Thus, the need for compatibility with the private sector to attain its support for the program may mean the expansion of public enterprise must await the development of a larger private sector. Secondly, a public sphere that showed a trend of continuous enlargement at a steady pace would prove incompatible with the attraction of foreign private capital in the future to the extent that there is a tendency for private capital to avoid countries it fears are becoming "socialized."

There are several hindrances in Ireland to a course of action wherein the government would sell some of its public enterprises and create a revolving fund for use in new areas where the private economy has not shown initiative or interest. Such a course of action would not solve the marketing problems that Ireland faces in her attempt to expand exports unless new public enterprises performed better in this area than existing public enterprises. In the past the announcement that public stock would be sold to private buyers created political opposition from the Labor Party, and could lose support of this sector for the Program. Moreover, the private sector does not have the pool of managerial or technological resources to take over public enterprises on a large scale and operate them successfully.

These forces tend to circumscribe the future role of public enterprise in Ireland as an implementation tool for fulfillment of the 1970 goals of industrialization outlined in the Second Program, and point to the need for Ireland to consider the use of mixed public-private corporations as a dynamic tool for achieving increased exports, employment, and national income. There is precedent established for the mixed enterprise in Ireland, but it has not been given a positive role of any size as an implementation method for attaining plan objectives. There could be several advantages derived from the allotment of a larger role to the mixed public-private corporation within the government's kit of implementation tools. The mixed enterprise as opposed to the public enterprise would conserve on public funds; yet it would not necessarily dilute control of the direction of investment in accordance with the plan, since control of public investment by state companies is already, by the nature of the "independent" public enterprise, subject to centrifugal forces.

The establishment of mixed public-private enterprises with *foreign* capital could have at least two advantages in Ireland. Government funds used to attract external capital would not only create more new investment with a given amount of public funds than wholly-owned public enterprises, but would enlarge the source of capital available, lessening the need for domestic savings. In addition, mixed public-private enterprise combining government capital with foreign private ownership would be a way of tapping managerial ability, technological know-how, and marketing channels possessed by foreign firms. This would increase the efficiency of pounds invested by the government in industry inasmuch as there are deficiencies in these areas in present government corporations.

Subsidies

Government subsidies have been predominantly of two sorts: direct grants to industries undertaking investment that will contribute to plan goals, particularly the plan target of increased exports, and 100 per cent tax remission on new exports. Government grants have created resentment among the domestic business community. Tax subsidies have not as yet attracted comparable criticism or threatened to weaken the cooperative spirit of the plan as grants have done. For the most part, grants have gone to foreign firms, these same firms in most cases qualifying for subsidies in the form of tax remission as well. Some firms receiving grants have failed. The failures, the concentration of grants among foreign, tax-subsidized exporting firms, coupled with a general foreboding among the Irish concerning the efficiency and stability of industry attracted into an investment situation by grants, raise questions concerning the present administration of grants.

The development of the procedure of administering grants and tax remissions as co-equal prerequisites for the attraction of new investment apparently stemmed from the initial inability to anticipate relative reaction to these tools, the need to stimulate new industrial activity immediately, and the competitive precedent set by other countries and/or regions trying to attract foreign investors. There is the danger, as the two tools have worked together, of creating an enclave of foreign firms unable to compete in the domestic market, and contributing less than their potential to domestic economic development, while at the same time creating resentment from the Irish business community.

Evidence points to the facts that it is tax subsidies, not grants, that are important determinants of industry location in Ireland, and that the price of tax subsidy has not been inordinately high viewed from the standpoint of results achieved through its contribution to new investment and industrialization. A criticism must be voiced, however, that both of these subsidies distort the tax base, are not equitable, and hence not permanently desirable.

A further criticism appears warranted in the case of direct grants. The use of grants in Ireland would be most defensible in a case where they were used to underwrite initial expenses of setting up a new operation where such expenses would deter the small entrepreneur, especially since there is a need to see that no entrepreneurial potential lies fallow or underdeveloped. To achieve this defense in the Irish situation, the criteria used in awarding grants would have to be changed. Presently grants are administered primarily as though they were a vital factor in the location of new firms in Ireland, and hence a necessary complement to tax exemption, and less as a tool for encouraging domestic operations where alternative ways of financing are not available. Should a change be effected, it would diminish to a certain extent the problem of allowing foreign firms to compete in the domestic market since they would not be as heavily subsidized as presently. It would by no means solve this problem, however—a problem which must be met if Ireland enters the European Economic Community, since tariff barriers must be abolished and free trade established among members of this Community.

Government Credit

As an implementation tool government credit ranks high in regard to the conservation of public funds, and can be highly effective in stimulating new investment when it is given on subsidized terms in the form of low interest rates and/or lenient repayment periods. An active credit institution can often encourage new investment simply by guaranteeing new loans and/or standing ready to acquire debt or equity instruments not bought by the public. Moreover, a government credit agency with well-trained personnel can serve as a consulting center that functions to improve the business community's awareness of sound financial management procedures.

The potential of a dynamic credit policy by the government has not been tapped in Ireland, and government credit has been of less significance within the mix of implementation tools than grants, tax exemption, or government enterprise. The problem has not been one of a shortage of capital; rather, the reason lies within the choice of the Industrial Credit Company as the main agent for carrying out government industrial credit policies. The Industrial Credit Company has exhibited a relatively conservative, traditional approach to credit availability, looking to its profit and loss position in priority to the risk assumptions needed within the domestic Irish economy to encourage long-range goals of large increases in industrial activity and managerial development.

The government has set up a new credit institution to be managed by the Industrial Credit Company which will be responsible for large loans to one business where the need for the business in relation to planning policies is important. This new agency was designed to deal with a specific project for aircraft manufacturing, and allows government equity participation in lieu of loan repayment. There are not any plans to increase funds available in this manner on a large scale with the purpose of encouraging mixed public-private investment ventures. Thus, the positive role that could be played by mixed enterprises has escaped attention.

THE FUTURE

Can Ireland rely upon the implementation tools that have served her well in the past six years to carry her through to the goals of 1970 and beyond? Will the relative roles of the individual components of the mix of tools need to be changed, or will new tools have to be added to capitalize upon the momentum of expansion built up with the success of planning to date? Can

Ireland improve upon the economic costs of goal attainment through improvement of the efficiency of the implementation tools used?

There is no reason to believe that tax exemption, which has a large drawing power, and relatively high efficiency rating, cannot continue to lure firms to Ireland's shores. Through attracting foreign firms with marketing channels other than in the United Kingdom, tax exemption can help to diversify Ireland's export markets and reduce her dependence upon demand conditions in one market. The forecast lowering of world-wide air freight rates will place Ireland in an improved position for attracting export firms, and contribute to the continued success of the Shannon Industrial Estate.[1] Also, resentment of further build-ups of American ownership in certain European countries could divert investment to Ireland to retain European markets.

A decline in male-female wage differentials within Ireland, and differentials in wages between Ireland and Europe, could diminish new foreign investment to a degree. However, if tight labor markets and pressure for higher wages continue in Europe, and the OECD has forecast that this will be the case, then the effect of somewhat higher wages in Ireland would not be detrimental to new investment. Moreover, higher worker incomes could improve domestic demand and enlarge the market in Ireland. Inflation is not a current problem of magnitude, and the Irish are constantly alert to avoid its development. Wages, foreign markets, and tax exemption should be able to continue to offer the new investor a reason for coming to Ireland.

Tax exemption has also helped to induce domestic firms to orient their thinking toward exporting, and seek new investment projects that will increase Ireland's sales of industrial products to overseas customers. The government, as evidenced in the Second Program, appears ready to extend the period over which tax exemption affects export profits in order to attract new firms by a ten-year exemption period. While there is the danger that an undue period of exemption will undermine the tax base needed to provide infrastructure for an expanding economy, at the present time there is not a shortage of government capital to the extent that it would inhibit needed expansion in telephone service, power needs, transportation, etc. In addition, by 1968 those firms that started export production in 1958 will begin their tapering-off period and start to pay taxes, and five years thereafter, must pay taxes at the full rate on profits. Statistics of this study indicate, however, that a period of 25 years of full tax relief such as provided by the Shannon Estate is not necessary to attract new investment in accordance with plan needs. This period of exemption appears more questionable now than at the inception of operations at Shannon in 1958, when there were few external economies in the area.

Credit could come forward into a prominant position among the implementation tools in Ireland, replacing grants and conserving on government funds in the process. Before this could occur, however, there would have to be a metamorphosis of the Industrial Credit Company. Or, alternatively, a development bank would have to be set up ready to take risks at subsidized interest rates on the chance that aggregate performance of the economy, particularly the domestic business sector, would bring long-run returns above costs. There is a need for an implementation tool such as lenient credit to retain the domestic economy's support of planning and enable it to move forward as the foreign and public sectors move forward. A failure to keep pace would wreck the cooperative spirit of planning and bring failure to the participant planning experience in Ireland. Now, prior to entry into the European Economic Community, is the time to build up the strength of the private domestic sector.

The foreign and public sectors' relative roles *vis-a-vis* the domestic private sector are tied in with the potential trouble spot of a non-responding domestic sector. The mixed public-private enterprise, combined with domestic and with foreign capital, could bring about a blurring of the sectoral divisions and avoid the potential this division holds for disruptive repercussions upon the democratic support of planning. Not only would mixed enterprises decrease the criticisms of the government for giving large grants to foreign firms without having a stake in the business, but it would improve upon the conservation of government funds over wholly-owned public enterprise. Moreover, equity ownership by a well-staffed government development bank could provide the government with an opportunity to educate domestic businessmen in financial management and other management areas.

If credit markets should tighten with the progress of expansion, the need for allocation of credit among strategic areas of investment would demand a more detailed priority rating of new investment than exists under current planning methodology. It is unlikely, however, given Ireland's financial rating with international lending institutions, her ability to attract foreign capital, and her savings rate trend, that credit will tighten to the extent that a plan to provide easy credit to domestic businesses would have to be curtailed. Also, funds formally given in grants could be diverted to credit agencies. Thus, the use of credit in a more imaginative manner, and the introduction of a dynamic role for the mixed enterprise would fit in with the type of planning adopted in Ireland, and play the important role of preventing the domination of the economy by an enclave of foreign firms. Failure to integrate the economy will diminish the potential returns to be received from tax remission on exports received by foreign firms.

THE HOPE OF PROGRESS

Certainly the success of Ireland's industrialization is not assured by its current progress. Ireland has only lessened, not solved her emigration and unemployment problems—two major incentives for inaugurating planning, and important determinants of how successful her planning efforts have been. Nor has the planning endeavor set the domestic economy firmly on its feet. However, continued progress is feasible as a result of the groundwork laid from 1958 to 1964. A relapse into the suffocating pessimism of the past would pose more of a hurdle than does Ireland's scarcity of natural resources. A lack of support for planning from domestic businessmen and workers could present a greater threat to industrial expansion than a raising of British tariffs. A strong resentment of foreign industry or the failure to orient her educational system toward her economic needs could offset the potential advantages that can come with drastic reductions of air freight costs.

Confidence to proceed without fear and doubt is possibly the greatest gain to come from Ireland's initial success in planning. Hopefully, the new-found confidence is built on a sturdy foundation of faith in progress so that some sideslips or backslides along the future path will not dilute the spirit of forward drive. As J. D. Bury has noted, in the scheme of thought the idea of progress has emerged late in history, although it may shape history at a pace to overcome effects of its tardiness.[2] The Irish slept as the world around them moved past, and the contrast in living standards drove out thousands from the island each year who wished to move with the forces of progress. Irish literature is replete with the plaintive notes struck upon the chords of discontent of a people scattered and discouraged. The time arrived when this nation of rich heritage, which helped to keep learning alive in the Middle Ages, found its future threatened, and awakened to the desires of the people to move apace of civilization as it is defined today. Of course, conflicting ideas exist among the Irish in regard to what exactly the content of progress is, and how much of this content is composed of material advancement. But few things could please the combative Irish more than an opportunity for vigorous dispute on a subject permeated with philosophical overtones. And midst the "big fuss" changes of lasting impact are taking place.

Notes

1. The head economic planner at Lockheed-Georgia Company forecasts vast declines in the cost of shipping by air, totaling in certain cases up to 50 per cent of present costs. This information was obtained in a private interview.

2. J. D. Bury, *The Idea of Progress*, New York: Dover Publications, Inc., 1955. As Bury points out, this idea is so much a part of our background we do not realize it is modern in origin, and that the Greeks, Romans, or Medieval and Renaissance Europeans were not accustomed to the concept. It was a product of the Enlightenment.

BIBLIOGRAPHY

PUBLICATIONS OF THE REPUBLIC OF IRELAND

An Foras Tionscal (Grant Board). *Annual Reports 1955-1964.*

Beddy, Dr. J. P. *Aspects of Industrial Banking.* An address delivered to the members of the British Institute of Management in Glasgow on 12th February, 1964. Dublin: Industrial Credit Co., Ltd.

Budget 1963. Dublin: Stationery Office, 1963.

Capital Budget 1964. Dublin: Stationery Office, 1964.

Capital Investment Advisory Committee. *Third Report.* Dublin: Stationery Office, circa 1958.

Central Statistics Office. *Irish Trade Journal and Statistical Bulletin,* XXXVIII (September, 1963).

Central Statistics Office. *National Income and Expenditure 1962.* Dublin: Stationery Office, 1963.

Central Statistics Office. *Trade Statistics of Ireland, February 1964.* Dublin: Stationery Office, 1964.

Central Statistics Office. *Statistical Abstract of Ireland, 1964.* Dublin: Stationery Office, 1964.

Committee on Industrial Organization. *Industry Reports.* Dublin: Stationery Office, 1963.

Department of Industry and Commerce. Industrial Reorganization Branch, *Guide to Principal Forms of State Aids and Services for Irish Industry.* Dublin: Department of Industry and Commerce, January, 1964.

Economic Development. Dublin: Stationery Office, 1958.

Economic Statistics Issued Prior to the Budget 1963. Dublin: Stationery Office, 1963.

Fennell, Rosemary. *Industrialization and Agricultural Development In The Congested Districts.* Dublin: *An Foras Taluntais* (Rural Economy Division), April, 1962.

First Program For Economic Expansion. Dublin: Stationery Office, 1958.

The Industrial Credit Company, Ltd. *Annual Reports, 1958-1964.* Dublin: ICC.

The Industrial Credit Company, Ltd. *Capital for Industry.* Dublin: ICC, circa 1958.

Industrial Development Authority. *Manufacturing in Ireland.* Dublin: I. D. A., circa 1959.

Industrial Development Authority. *Opportunities for Industrialists.* Dublin: I.D.A., circa 1960.

Industrial Development (Encouragement of External Investment) Act, 1958. Dublin: Stationery Office, 1958.

The Irish Export Board. *Annual Reports, 1957-1964.* Dublin: *Coras Trachtala.*

National Industrial Economic Council. *Interim Reports.* Dublin: Stationery Office (issued at varying intervals since 1958).

National Industrial Economic Council. *Report on Procedures for Continuous Review of Progress Under the Second Program for Economic Expansion.* Dublin: Stationery Office, June, 1964.

National Industrial Economic Council. *Report on Results of Discussions With Industry on the Second Program Targets.* Dublin: Stationery Office, November, 1964.

National Industrial Economic Council. *Report on Results of Discussions With Industry on the Second Program Targets.* 1965.

Program of Sea Fisheries Development. Dublin: Stationery Office, 1962.

Progress Reports on the Program for Economic Expansion. (Issued every 6 months.) Dublin: Stationery Office.

Second Program for Economic Expansion, Part I. Dublin: Stationery Office, 1963.

Second Program for Economic Expansion, Part II. Dublin: Stationery Office, 1964.

Shannon Free Airport Development Company, Ltd. *Annual Reports, 1962 and 1963.* Shannon: Shannon Free Airport Development Co., Ltd.

BOOKS

Abramovitz, Moses, *et. al. The Allocation of Economic Resources.* Stanford: Stanford University Press, 1959.

Bury, J. D. *The Idea of Progress.* New York: Dover Publications, Inc., 1955.

Clark, Colin. *The Conditions of Economic Progress.* 3rd ed. London: Mc-Millan and Company, Ltd., 1957.

Clark, J. M. *Demobilization of Wartime Economic Controls.* New York: Mc-Graw-Hill Book Co., Inc., 1944.

Dahl, Robert A., and Lindblom, Charles E. *Politics, Economics and Welfare.* New York: Harper and Brothers, 1953.

DeHaven, J. C., Hirshleifer, Jack, and Milliman, J. W. *Water Supply, Economic Technology and Policy.* Chicago: University of Chicago Press. 1960.

Eckstein, Otto, and Krutilla, J. V. *Multiple Purpose River Development.* Baltimore: Johns Hopkins Press, 1958.

Eckstein, Otto. *Water Resource Development.* Boston: Harvard University Press, 1958.

Enke, Stephen. *Economics for Development.* Englewood Cliffs, N. J: Prentice-Hall, Inc., 1963.

Fitzgerald, Garret. *State Sponsored Bodies.* Dublin: Institute of Public Administration, 1963.

Goode, Richard. "Taxation and Economic Development," *Readings in Economic Development.* Morgan, *et. al.,* eds. Belmont, California: Wadsworth Publishing Co., Inc., 1963.

Hackett, Anne-Marie, and Hackett, John. *Economic Planning in France.* London: George Allen and Unwin, Ltd., 1963.

Hanson, A. H. *Public Enterprise and Economic Development*. London: Routledge and Kegan Paul, Ltd., 1959.

Higgins, Benjamin. *Economic Development*. New York: W. W. Norton and Company, Inc., 1959.

Hirschman, A. O. *The Strategy of Economic Development*. New Haven, Connecticut: Yale University Press, 1960.

Hoselitz, B. F., and More, W. E., eds. *Industrialization and Society*. New York: Unesco-Mouton, 1963.

J. Walter Thompson Company. *The Western European Markets*. New York: McGraw-Hill Book Company, Inc., 1957.

Kuznets, S., Moore, W., and Spengler, J. J., eds. *Economic Growth: Brazil, India, Japan*. Durham, North Carolina: Duke University Press, 1955.

Lepawsky, Albert. *State Planning and Economic Development in the South*. Washington: National Planning Association, 1949.

Lewis, John P. *Quiet Crisis in India*. Washington, D.C.: The Brookings Institute, 1962.

Lewis, W. Arthur. *The Principles of Economic Planning*. Washington: Public Affairs Press, 1951.

Lewis, W. Arthur. *The Theory of Economic Growth*. Homewood, Illinois: Richard D. Irwin, Inc., 1955.

Mason, Edward S. *Economic Planning In Underdeveloped Areas: Government and Business*. New York: Fordham University Press, 1958.

McLaughlin, G. E., and Robock, Stefan H. *Why Industry Moves South*. Washington: National Planning Association, 1949.

Moes, John E. *Local Subsidies for Industry*. Chapel Hill, North Carolina: University of North Carolina Press, 1962.

Morgan, T., Betz, G. W., and Choudbry, N. K., eds. *Readings in Economic Development*. Belmont, California: Wadsworth Publishing Co., Inc., 1963.

Myrdal, Gunnar. *Economic Theory and Underdeveloped Regions*. London: Gerald Duckworth and Company, Ltd., 1957.

O'Mahony, David. *The Irish Economy.* Cork: Cork University Press, 1964.

Rostow, W. W. *The Stages of Economic Growth.* New York: Cambridge University Press, 1960.

Shannon, Lyle W., ed. *Underdeveloped Areas, A Book of Readings and Research.* New York: Harper and Brothers, 1957.

Sheahan, John. *Promotion and Control of Industry in Postwar France.* Cambridge, Massachusetts: Harvard University Press, 1963.

Smith, Thomas C. *Political Change and Industrialization in Japan: Government Enterprise, 1868-1880.* Stanford: Stanford University Press, 1955.

Stead, William H. *Fomento—The Economic Development of Puerto Rico.* Washington: National Planning Association, 1958.

Taylor, Milton C. *Industrial Tax Exemption in Puerto Rico.* Madison, Wisconsin: University of Wisconsin Press, 1957.

Tinbergen, Jan. *Central Planning.* New Haven, Connecticut: Yale University Press, 1964.

Tinbergen, Jan. *The Design of Development.* Baltimore: The Johns Hopkins Press, 1958.

JOURNALS

Administration, Bord Na Mona (Special Issue) 7 (Spring, 1959).

Baldwin, G. B. "Public Enterprise in Indian Industry," *Pacific Affairs,* 30 (March, 1957), 3-21

Chenery, H. B. "The Application of Investment Criteria," *Quarterly Journal of Economics,* LVII (February, 1953), 76-96.

Chenery, H. B. "Comparative Advantage and Development Policy," *American Economic Review,* LI (March, 1961), 158-186.

Goffman, I. J., and Thompson, J. H. "Replies and Rejoinder," *Southern Economic Journal,* XXIX (October, 1962), 111-126.

Isard, Walter, and Schooler, Eugene W. "Industrial Complex Analysis, Agglomerate Economics, and Regional Development," *Journal of Regional
Science,* I (Spring, 1959), 19-33.

Kahn, A. E. "Investment Criteria in Development," *Quarterly Journal of
Economics,* LV (February, 1951), 38-61.

Lemass, S. F. "The Role of the State-Sponsored Bodies in the Economy,"
Administration (Dublin), 6 (Winter, 1958-59), 277-295.

Linehan, T. P. "The Structure of Irish Industry," *Journal of the Statistical
and Social Inquiry Society of Ireland,* 1961-62, 220-253.

Lynch, P. "Economic Planning in Ireland," *Administration* (Dublin), 8 (August,
1960), 181-190.

Moes, John E. "Subsidization of Industry by Local Communities in the South,"
Southern Economic Journal, XXVIII (October, 1961), 187-193.

Rae, Arthur. "Adaptation Councils at Work," *Journal of the Irish Management
Institute,* II (February, 1964), 68-72.

Robock, Stefan H. "Industrialization and Economic Progress in the Southeast," *Southern Economic Journal,* XX (April, 1954), 307-327.

Scully, M. "Parliamentary Control of Public Corporations in Eire," *Public
Administration,* XXXII (Winter, 1954), 455-462.

Stock, Leon O. "Operation 'Eire Lift,'" *Taxes—The Tax Magazine,* XLI
(November, 1963), 662-671.

Wellisz, Stanislaw. "Economic Planning in the Netherlands, France, and
Italy," *Journal of Political Economy,* LXVIII (June, 1960), 252-283.

INFORMATION SOURCES IN IRELAND

An Foras Tionscal (Grant Board)

Central Statistics Office.

Coras Tractala (Export Board).

Department of Finance.

Department of Industry and Commerce: Technical Assistance Branch and Industrial Reorganization Branch.

The Economic Research Institute.

Federation of Irish Industries.

Industrial Credit Company, Limited.

Industrial Development Authority.

Revenue Commission.

Shannon Free Airport Development Company, Limited.

Trinity College.

OTHER SOURCES

"Keeping Steam in Mexico's Boom," *Business Week,* November 28, 1964.

CEPES (The European Committee for Economic and Social Progress). *French and Other National Economic Plans for Growth.* Paris: *CEPES,* June, 1963.

The Federation of Irish Industries. *Industrial Review,* March-April, 1964.

The Financial Times. "Republic of Ireland: A Financial Times Survey," April 11, 1960.

IMEDE (l'Institut pour l'Etude des Methodes de Direction de l'Entreprise). *Economic Planning in France.* Lausanne, Switzerland, 1962.

Irish Times. "Irish Review and Annual 1962," Supplement to the *Irish Times,* January 1, 1963.

Lewis, John P. *Notes on the Nurture of Country Planning.* Bulletin published by the Bureau of Business Research, Graduate School of Business, Indiana University, Bloomington, Indiana, 1962.

OECD (Organization for Economic Cooperation and Development). *Ireland,* Paris: OECD, annual issues 1962, 1963, and 1964.

Papanek, G. F., and Quresh, M. A. "The Use of Accounting Prices in Planning," *Organization, Planning and Programming for Economic Development.* Washington: U.S. Government Printing Office, 1964.

Republic of France. *The Fourth Modernization and Equipment Plan, Statements Before the National Assembly.* French Affairs, No. 139. June, 1962.

Republic of France. *French Economic Planning.* French Affairs, No. 127, December, 1961.

Roterus, Victor. "Community Industrial Development—A Nationwide Survey," U. S. Congress, Senate Committee on Banking and Currency. *Development Corporations and Authorities.* 86th Congress, 1st Session. Washington: U.S. Government Printing Office, December, 1959.

Ryan, W. J. L. *Investment Criteria in Ireland.* A paper read before the Society on November 17, 1961. Cahill and Company, Ltd., Dublin, Ireland.

Time Magazine. 82, July 12, 1963, 28-40.

The Times (London). *Review of Industry,* January, 1963.

United Nations. *World Economic Survey 1959.* New York: U.N., 1960.

United States Bureau of the Budget. *Measuring Productivity of Federal Government Organizations.* Washington, D. C.: U.S. Government Printing Office, 1964.

United States. *Organization, Planning, and Programming for Economic Development,* VIII. U. S. Papers Prepared for the United Nations Conference on the Application of Science and Technology for the Benefit of the Less Developed Areas. Washington: U. S. Government Printing Office, 1964.